Quick Reference to
Nursing Leadership

Delmar Publishers' Online Services

To access Delmar on the World Wide Web, point your browser to:
http://www.delmar.com/delmar.html
To access through Gopher: gopher://gopher.delmar.com
(Delmar Online is part of "thomson.com," an Internet site with information on more than 30 publishers of the International Thomson Publishing organization.)
For information on our products and services:
email: info@delmar.com
or call 800-347-7707

Quick Reference to
Nursing Leadership

Donna M. Costello-Nickitas, RN, PhD
Associate Professor and Graduate Specialty Coordinator,
 Nursing Administration
Hunter College, CUNY
New York, New York

Delmar Publishers

 An International Thomson Publishing Company

Albany • Bonn • Boston • Cincinnati • Detroit • London
Madrid • Melbourne • Mexico City • New York • Pacific Grove • Paris
San Francisco • Singapore • Tokyo • Toronto • Washington

NOTICE TO THE READER

Publisher does not warrant or guarantee any of the products described herein or perform any independent analysis in connection with any of the product information contained herein. Publisher does not assume, and expressly disclaims, any obligation to obtain and include information other than that provided to it by the manufacturer.

The reader is expressly warned to consider and adopt all safety precautions that might be indicated by the activities herein and to avoid all potential hazards. By following the instructions contained herein, the reader willingly assumes all risks in connection with such instructions.

The publisher makes no representation or warranties of any kind, including but not limited to, the warranties of fitness for particular purpose or merchantability, nor are any such representations implied with respect to the material set forth herein, and the publisher takes no responsibility with respect to such material. The publisher shall not be liable for any special, consequential, or exemplary damages resulting, in whole or part, from the readers' use of, or reliance upon, this material.

Delmar Staff
Acquisitions Editor: Bill Burgower
Assistant Editor: Hilary A. Schrauf
Project Editor: Judith Boyd Nelson

Production Coordinator: Barbara A. Bullock
Art and Design Coordinator: Carol D. Keohane
Cover Design: The Drawing Board

COPYRIGHT © 1997 By Delmar Publishers
a division of International Thomson Publishing Inc.
The ITP logo is a trademark under license.
Printed in the United States of America

For more information, contact:
Delmar Publishers
3 Columbia Circle, Box 15015
Albany, New York 12212-5015

International Thomson Publishing Europe
Berkshire House 168-173
High Holborn
London, WC1V 7AA
England

Thomas Nelson Australia
102 Dodds Street
South Melbourne, 3205
Victoria, Australia

Nelson Canada
1120 Birchmont Road
Scarborough, Ontario
Canada, M1K 5G4

International Thomson Editores
Campos Eliseos 385, Piso 7
Col Polanco
11560 Mexico D F Mexico

International Thomson Publishing GmbH
Konigswinterer Strasse 418
53227 Bonn
Germany

International Thomson Publishing Asia
221 Henderson Road
#05-10 Henderson Building
Singapore 0315

International Thomson Publishing—Japan
Hirakawacho Kyowa Building, 3F
2-2-1 Hirakawacho
Chiyoda-ku, Tokyo 102
Japan

All rights reserved. No part of this work covered by the copyright hereon may be reproduced or used in any form or by any means—graphic, electronic, or mechanical, including photocopying, recording, taping, or information storage and retrieval systems—without the written permission of the publisher.

2 3 4 5 6 7 8 9 10 XXX 02 01 00 99 98 97 96

Library of Congress Cataloging-in-Publication Data
Costello-Nickitas, Donna M.
   Quick reference to nursing leadership / Donna M. Costello
-Nickitas.
      p. cm. — (Delmar quick reference series in nursing
administration)
   Includes bibliographical references and index.
   ISBN 0-8273-6997-2
   1. Nursing services—Administration.   2. Leadership.   I. Title.
II. Series.
   [DNLM: 1. Nursing Supervisory—organization & administration
—handbooks.   2. Leadership—handbooks.   WY 49 C841q 1997]
RT89.C34   1997
362.1'73'068—dc20
DNLM/DLC
for Library of Congress

96-12506
CIP

*To my husband, Michael, and my children,
Nick, Catherine, and Jon-Philip, who taught me the true
meaning of love, service, and commitment,
the keys to successful leadership*

**Delmar Quick Reference Series
in Nursing Administration**
Ruth Alward, Series Editor

Quick Reference to Nursing Leadership
Donna M. Costello-Nickitas, PhD, RN

**Quick Reference to Redesigning
the Nursing Organization**
Mary L. Fisher, PhD, RN, CNAA

**Quick Reference for Directors of Nursing
in Long-Term Care**
Ethel L. Mitty, EdD, RN

Introduction to the Quick Reference Series

This book is part of a series of quick reference volumes for the busy nurse administrator and manager. Regardless of education and experience, there are many occasions when you need to turn to a reference book in your normal workday or as you begin a new position, a new project, or a new committee assignment. Rather than having to consult more generalized nursing administration textbooks, you can now turn to books designed to be easily accessible and practical, featuring helpful tables and figures as well as examples of approaches that work.

Each volume in the Quick Reference Series is targeted to meeting the need for pertinent information on the topics you have identified as important to your management practice. Nursing administration students will also find the series instructive.

We are committed to providing excellence in the content, format, and usability of the Quick Reference Series.

Ruth R. Alward, EdD, RN
Series Editor
President, Nurse Executive Associates, Inc.
Washington, DC

Contributors

Martin Dornbaum, MS, BCOA
Fellow and Director
Helene Fuld Media/Learning Center
Hunter College Bellevue School of Nursing
New York, New York

Mary Ellen Lorefice, MSW
Private Practice
Old Greenwich, Connecticut

Contents

Quick Reference Topics   xiv
List of Figures   xviii
Preface   xix
Acknowledgments   xxi
Foreword   xxii

CHAPTER 1 *Leadership versus Management*   1
Distinguishing between Leadership and Management   3
The Leadership Impact   6
Leadership and Nursing: A Perfect Match   8
Strategies for Leading   10
Summary   13
References   14

CHAPTER 2 *A Shift in the Leadership Paradigm*   15
The Changing Nature of Leadership   15
Feminine Approaches and Expectations   18
Turning Reality on Its Head   21
Challenges and Obstacles   23
Reshaping Leadership   25
Summary   26
References   26

CHAPTER 3 *The Three P's of Leadership: Power, Politics, and Policy*   28
Becoming Political and Powerful   29

Walking the Power Line   31
The Art of Negotiating   32
Workplace Politics and Policy   35
How to Influence Policy   37
The Policy Checklist   38
Summary   41
References   41

CHAPTER 4 *Expanding the Power Universe*   42

A Shared Responsibility   42
From Power to Empowerment   43
The Empowerment Model   46
Learning to Surrender Control   48
Creating Self-Directed Teams   49
Collective Decision Making   50
Summary   55
References   55

CHAPTER 5 *Teamwork: A Leader's Solution*   57

Why Teamwork?   57
The Vision   60
   Defining the Vision   60
   Creating a Vision   61
   Moving the Vision to Action   62
Team Leadership   62
Definition of a Team   65
Team Building   66
Creating a Winning Team   70
Securing Commitment   70
   Give Feedback   71
   Give Recognition   72
   Give Rewards   72
Summary   72
References   73

CHAPTER 6 *Understanding Change*   75

The Change Process   75
Becoming a Change Agent   76
Laying the Groundwork   77

Planting the Seed   79
Creating a Change Strategy   80
Using Communication   81
The Human Aspect   82
A Shift in Mind-Set   84
Change and Problem Solving   85
Celebrating Change   86
Summary   86
References   90

CHAPTER 7 *Facilitating the Group Process*   91

The Nature of Group Work   92
Becoming a Facilitator   93
The Art of Facilitation   93
   Facilitating Feelings   94
   The Facilitator's Role   95
   Promoting Group Openness and Participation   96
   Direct Question   96
   General Question   96
   Return Question   96
   Relay Question   96
   Seeking Consensus and Managing Differences   97
Group Meetings   99
   Preparation   99
Meeting Dynamics   101
Resolving Conflict   101
Facilitator Responsibilities   105
Summary   106
References   106

CHAPTER 8 *Human Resources Management*   107

Forging a Partnership   108
Market-Focused Leadership   109
Moving People, Making Opportunities   111
   Mentoring   112
   Networking   113
   Maintaining Marketability   114
The Hiring Process   115
   The Resumé   115
   The Cover Letter   118

The Interview   119
Preparing for the Interview   121
Ten Questions to Avoid   122
Red Flags   123

Summary   123

References   124

CHAPTER 9 *Fostering a Caring Workplace*   125

BY MARY ELLEN LOREFICE AND DONNA M. COSTELLO-NICKITAS

Healthy Leaders, Healthy Communication   125

Caring and Supportive Leader Behaviors   126

Understanding Communication   128
   The Message   129
   The Audience   129

Becoming an Effective Communicator   130

Problem Solving   133

Rekindling the Workplace   135

Summary   137

References   137

CHAPTER 10 *Time Management*   139

Getting Started   139

Staying Focused   141

One Step at a Time   143
   Living by the Calendar   145
   The Daily List   145
   High-Peak Activities   147
   Low-Peak Activities   147

Pushing Priorities, Eliminating Wasters   147

Becoming a Time Saver   148
   Delegate   148
   Prioritize Activities   149

Making Tracks   151
   Team Member Time   151
   Peer and Colleague Time   151
   Boss Time   152

Keeping Track   152

Evaluating Progress   153

Summary   153

References   154

CHAPTER 11 *Performance Measurement* 155

Motivation and Performance 156
Performance Systems 158
   Job Descriptions 158
   Principles of Performance Management 159
   The Performance Dialogue 160
   Key Elements of Performance Measurement 161
Creating a Support System 162
   Nurse Leader Support 162
   Team Support 163
   Nurse Leader–Team Support 163
Feedback 163
Successful Performance and Rewards 167
Summary 168
References 169

CHAPTER 12 *Computer Technology and Nursing Leadership* 170

BY DONNA M. COSTELLO-NICKITAS AND MARTIN DORNBAUM

Nursing Applications 171
Computer Applications 172
   Nursing Information Systems 173
   Hospital Information Systems 173
   Decision Support Systems 173
   Executive Information Systems 174
Nurses on the Internet 175
   Traveling the Internet 175
   Learning the Language 175
On-Line Networks for Nursing 177
Databases for Nursing Professionals 177
Research Publications and Databases 178
Summary 178
References 179

APPENDIX A **WORKSHEET FOR DESIGNING A PLANNED CHANGE** 180
APPENDIX B **DIRECTORY OF NATIONAL NURSING ORGANIZATIONS** 184
APPENDIX C **COMPUTER SOFTWARE FOR NURSE LEADERS** 188
GLOSSARY 190
INDEX 193

Quick Reference Topics

CHAPTER 1 *Leadership versus Management*
- How to Sharpen Self-Knowledge Skills   2
- How to Encourage High Morale and Esprit de Corps   6
- Interpersonal Skills of Leadership   7
- Steps for Promoting a Personal Best among Followers   7
- The Roles of Leaders   9

CHAPTER 2 *A Shift in the Leaderhip Paradigm*
- Qualities of Feminine Leadership   17
- Core Elements of Feminine Leadership   19
- Goal of Feminine Leadership   20
- Strategies for Balancing System Goals with Interpersonal Relationships   21
- Skills and Strategies of Feminine Leadership   23
- Behaviors of Feminine Leadership   25
- Caring in Nursing   25

CHAPTER 3 *The Three P's of Leadership: Power, Politics, and Policy*
- The Building Blocks of Political Savvy   29
- Political Behavior for the Workplace   30
- Ways to Broaden Support and Work Collectively with Others   30
- The Power Walk   31
- Being an Effective, Influential Negotiator   32
- Being an Image Maker   34
- Key Elements of the Organization System   35
- Power Broker Techniques and Strategies   35
- Playing by the Organization Rules   36

Lessons on Raising Your Voice   37
Making a Policy Checklist   39
Strategies for Advancing Policy Initiatives   39
Turning Ideas into Political Realities   40

CHAPTER 4 *Expanding the Power Universe*

Attributes that Build Empowerment   44
How to Promote Professional Development   45
Empowerment Model Goals   46
Sharing Control   48
Strategies for Creating Self-Directed Teams   49
Work Restructuring   51
Key Behaviors of Empowerment   54

CHAPTER 5 *Teamwork: A Leader's Solution*

Components of Patient-Centered Care   58
How to Establish Effective Nursing Teams   58
Techniques to Keep the Team Rolling   59
How to Create a Vision   61
Qualities for Building or Redesigning a High-Performance Team   62
The Keys to Team Building   65
The Benefits of Teamwork   67
Strategies for Managing Teams   71

CHAPTER 6 *Understanding Change*

Principles of Change   76
Tips on Facilitating Change   77
How to Demonstrate Change Is Needed   79
Tips for Creating a Winning Strategy   80
The Communication Plan   81
Key Elements for Mapping Change   84
The Problem-Solving Process   86

CHAPTER 7 *Facilitating the Group Process*

Qualities of Primary Facilitators   91
Measuring Group Effectiveness   91

Group Variables 92
The Facilitator's Role 93
Behaviors Essential to Group Process 95
Strategies for Ensuring Harmony 97
Facilitating Diversity 98
Conflict Resolution Styles 102
Seven Steps to Conflict Resolution 103
Dealing with the People Who Cause Conflict 104
Leader Responsibilities 105

CHAPTER 8 *Human Resources Management*

Mobilizing Human Resources: Vision and Values 107
Understanding the Organization's Purpose and Business 111
Activities for Maintaining Visibility 114
Writing a Resumé 116
Guidelines for an Effective Interview 120
Sample Interview Questions 120
Meeting the Job Applicant 121

CHAPTER 9 *Fostering a Caring Workplace*

Supportive Nurse Leader Behaviors 126
Being Trustworthy and Reliable 127
Modeling Respectful Behavior 127
How to Promote Positive Interaction 128
How to Become an Effective Communicator 130
Dealing with Resistance to Change 133
Problem-Solving Communication Skills 134

CHAPTER 10 *Time Management*

A Sample Mission Statement 141
Components of Goal Formulation 142
Creating an Action Plan 143
Categorizing Priorities 146
How to Delegate Effectively 149
First Things First 150

CHAPTER 11 *Performance Measurement*

Role Responsibilities   155
Questions to Guide Performance Measurement   158
Opening the Performance Evaluation Dialogue   160
Benefits of Continuous Feedback   165
Potential Rewards and Recognitions   168

CHAPTER 12 *Computer Technology and Nursing Leadership*

How to Implement Information Technology   170
Benefits of Information Systems   174

List of Figures

Chapter 1 *Leadership versus Management*
Figure 1.1   Differences between Leaders and Managers   4

Chapter 2 *A Shift in the Leadership Paradigm*
Figure 2.1   Style and Characteristics of Feminine Leadership   18

Chapter 5 *Teamwork: A Leader's Solution*
Figure 5.1   Personal Effectiveness Profile   64
Figure 5.2   Team Readiness Checklist   67
Figure 5.3   Team Performance Worksheet   70
Figure 5.4   Workplace Motivation Factors Inventory   71

Chapter 6 *Understanding Change*
Figure 6.1   Mapping the Problem-Solving Process   88

Chapter 8 *Human Resources Management*
Figure 8.1   Putting the Resumé Together   116
Figure 8.2   Sample Chronological Resumé   117
Figure 8.3   Sample Cover Letter   118
Figure 8.4   Linking the Job Applicant to the Organization   119

Chapter 9 *Fostering a Caring Workplace*
Figure 9.1   Strategies to Foster Commitment   136

Chapter 10 *Time Management*
Figure 10.1   A Daily Time Log   140
Figure 10.2   Goal List   142
Figure 10.3   Sample Goal: Bite-Sized Units   142
Figure 10.4   Sample Mini–Filing Cabinet for Notebook   144
Figure 10.5   Sample Calendar   145

Preface

The dynamic health care environment has had a profound impact on the evolving role of nurse leaders. With the stark realities of the health care marketplace—the restructuring of hospitals, managed care, workforce redesign, collective bargaining, and fiscal constraints—nurse leaders have become the vital link between the larger vision of the health care organization and the unit-based system of patient care. To carry the organization's vision to the bedside, nurse leaders must make tough choices about resource allocation. Often the organization's success depends on these leaders' ability to provide insight into the priorities of patient care to the overall organization vision and mission. The commitment to meeting patient needs through excellence in clinical practice is the hallmark of nursing leadership.

Nurse leaders are accountable for setting a standard of excellence in clinical nursing practice and the delivery of patient care. This quick reference guide is designed to help nurse leaders in managing the functions, responsibilities, and decisions central to the delivery of quality patient care. Underlying the multiple responsibilities of nurse leaders are core values that influence and direct the distribution of human and fiscal resources, shape leadership style, and drive decisions. To be successful and productive, leaders must be able to respond quickly to changes in the market and disseminate information rapidly throughout their teams, using the talents of all team members.

To address the changing needs in health care delivery and provide the leadership necessary to restructure the system, I propose a contemporary feminine leadership style that emphasizes empowerment over power grabbing, self-management teams over command-and-control leadership, and continuous quality improvement over fixed blame. Feminine leadership seeks to encompass the values of wholeness, interconnectedness, equality, process, diversity, and collaboration. These core values are tied to women's ways of knowing, interacting, and decision making, and they stand in contrast to societal values of individualism, competition, and inequality.

Feminine leadership brings a new perspective to the organization, a different way of viewing the world. It provides insight about the world and shifts how we think, what we identify as pressing problems, and what solutions are most effective for these problems. Feminine leadership provides a new vision into how to confront the issues of power and freedom as well as what it means to be powerful and exercise power. This type of leadership values the gathering and giving of information as important components of the power equation. It prefers to share power, ask questions, engage in dialogue, encourage participation, and nurture self-esteem. This is not leadership as usual, with power controlled and information withheld.

Feminine leadership is transformational in nature. It will transform health care organizations into places that value and promote health as well as the bottom line and works towards collaborative solutions, including an understanding of the financial dimensions of the health care market.

By shifting from a traditional leadership style toward a nontraditional, feminine style, nurse leaders gain a new understanding of problem solving and decision making by listening until all voices reach consensus, recognizing diversity and multiculturalism in the expansion of frontiers of knowledge and change, and sharing power and information.

This book encompasses and appreciates the voices of women. The values that women leaders bring to the policy table are different from men and reflect an ethic of care that is inclusive and empowering. By using the skills and strategies suggested within these pages nurse leaders will develop new ways to influence, shape, and distribute human and fiscal resources. Most strategies are framed within the notion of inclusion; collaboration is encouraged and diversity and equality are highly valued in contrast to individualism, isolation, and competition.

Nurse leaders must be positioned to respond to the challenges and demands of a chaotic health care environment. This book emphasizes the wholeness and balance needed to meet the uncertainties of a reformed health care system. The focus on application of leadership strategies and skills rather than theory alone guides readers to understand, develop, and integrate leadership principles into professional practice.

Acknowledgments

No significant project or goal is ever accomplished in isolation. The concept of a quick reference guide for nurse leaders and the invitation to write about it comes from Dr. Ruth Alward. A friend and colleague, Ruth's support made this project a reality. From our days at Hunter College, we shared the rigorous lessons and requirements of preparing future nurse leaders.

To my friends of the Maher Ave. Book Club who believe that women's voices need to be heard in legitimate and meaningful ways, I thank you all for supporting my voice and vision for professional nurse leaders and for women leaders who step out into the public to raise their voices for those who cannot or for those who will not.

To Minette Nelson for her excellent proofreading abilities and willingness to assist at a moment's notice, thank you. I always appreciated her critical reviews, insights, and suggestions.

Special thanks go to Nancy Ward whose critical assistance and technological support in computer glitches was a saving grace. Nancy always had the right answers at the right time and in the right way.

Many thanks go to Mary Ellen Lorefice whose friendship and guidance on a daily basis nurtured this book to its final shape. Her continued encouragement and words of wisdom taught me how to be a servant leader. It was with Mary Ellen, along with Robin Horton, Tani Gazin, and Laura Parissi, that I also learned how truly to serve another while balancing the demands of family, work, and community.

I offer heartfelt appreciation to Hilary Schrauf, assistant editor, for her continued guidance and support through this project. I am grateful for her attention to detail and ability to transform ideas into concrete realities.

Finally, special thanks go to my husband, Michael, for his continued understanding, support, and appreciation of my work. He has learned to recognize the important contribution nurses and women make in our society. I am grateful for all of his encouragement and patience throughout this project.

Foreword

The health care system is undergoing unprecedented change, with two intersecting yet opposite variables coming together on a true collision course. On the one hand, advances in science are resulting in phenomenal technology, making it possible for health care providers to offer more and better care than ever before in human history. On the other hand, the economics of the day are requiring, and indeed forcing, cutbacks in services at every turn. As a consequence, everyone involved in health care is scrambling to find new structures and new delivery processes that can do more for less.

In this chaotic environment, the need for thoughtful, able leadership has never been greater. And nurses are in a strategic position because of their unique combination of knowlege and experience to provide vital contributions to leading the organizations in which they work.

In this book, Donna Costello-Nickitas offers practicing nurse managers important yet practical information on ways to transform their management roles into true leadership positions. The book is presented in a conceptual, clearly written style that reduces the material to concise, readily useable guidelines for busy professionals. Moreover, the content is tailored to the contemporary world of work and organizations. Today's environment offers many new challenges, and these require new approaches to leadership.

This book addresses current management needs and strategies in a direct and comprehensive fashion that will prove valuable to experienced and novice readers alike.

Margaret L. McClure, RN, EdD, FAAN
New York, New York

Chapter 1

Leadership versus Management

Leaders do the right thing. Managers do things right.
WARREN BENNIS AND BURT NANUS (1985)

You can learn the qualities and competencies required of a leader. But be aware that the leadership process is a human one, filled with risks, trial and error, intuition, and intellect.

Those who are attracted to leadership are often people who are willing to take charge, but taking charge and being responsible are not the only essential ingredients of **successful leadership**. Successful nurse leaders must also be:

- Flexible, to respond to changes in the workplace.
- Able to disseminate information rapidly throughout their teams.
- Able to develop trusting and strong interpersonal relationships with patients, peers, and other health care professionals.
- Able to build and support the talents and differences of all team members.
- Able to thrive on chaos and uncertainty.
- Builders of something that can grow and thereby help not only the organization but society as a whole.

Underlying the multiple responsibilities of the nurse leader are core values that influence and direct the distribution of human and fiscal resources. It is these values that shape the leadership style and drive the decisions made by today's nurse leaders.

This chapter outlines an old-fashioned philosophy about leadership: the belief that there are principles and values that encourage leadership to flourish, among them, trust, integrity, honesty, and commitment. These leadership principles are a part of the human condition.

> **TIP**
>
> The way to succeed as a leader is to create an atmosphere grounded in principles and values that seek to build trust: a trust inside yourself and trust in those you lead.

By creating an atmosphere of trust: you mean what you say—all your words and deeds are truthful and you believe in what you say—and all your actions speak the truth as well.

> **TIP**
>
> Do unto others as they would be done unto.

As a leader you will be judged on what you say and do. If you are principle centered, your leadership effectiveness does not change, regardless of external conditions or circumstances. You interpret and respond to all experiences with exactness, consistency, and strength.

Nurse leaders who aspire to transform the workplace environment understand that **leadership** is more than taking charge, holding a position of rank or authority, or having a title. It is knowing, applying, and improving on the core values and principles of who they are and what they want to accomplish, and trusting always on knowing what is right and necessary.

What can you do to meet the challenge of leadership?

How to Sharpen Self-Knowledge Skills

- **Become aware of and knowledgeable about your own core values and principles.**
- **Incorporate these values and principles into your leadership style and strategic plan.**
- **Keep abreast of and monitor your impact on human and fiscal resources management.**
- **Maximize your actions; for example, integrate the organization's mission into your personal core values with the purpose of influencing policy and program planning.**

- Articulate a concern for using the core values of trust, integrity, honesty, and commitment in the workplace. Show others how easily core values apply to the day-to-day business of clinical nursing.

> **TIP**
> Self-knowledge is the first step on the path to successful leadership.

Distinguishing between Leadership and Management

Although *leader* and *manager* are often used interchangeably in the workplace, these terms have important differences. Bennis and Nanus (1985), for example, say that leaders pull rather than push, inspire rather than order, and enable people to use their own initiative and experiences rather than deny or constrain those experiences and actions. In the labor-intensive environment of nursing service, nurse leaders must be prepared to balance the priorities of caring with the cost constraints of resources management, move from cooperation to collaboration, and promote clarity and precision in communication.

Bolman and Deal (1991) say that leaders (but not managers) know how to match the right idea to the right problem, at the right time, and in the right way. Nurse leaders must match the larger vision of the health care organization and the unit-based system of patient care at the right time and in the right way. In helping others to influence and shape the organization, they ensure that the goals of caring and efficiency are balanced. This balance of carefully managing the cost/care equation distinguishes nurse leaders from traditional, bureaucratic leaders.

Nurse leaders have to learn to manage in situations in which they do not have command and authority and are neither controlled nor controlling. This leadership role is dictated by today's new way of doing business in a competitive patient-focused environment.

> **TIP**
> Nurse leaders must continually demonstrate the courage and commitment to keep patients and the community first on the list of health care priorities.

Leaders, says DePree (1989), are responsible for fostering environments and work processes within which people can develop high-quality relationships—relationships with each other, relationships with groups with which they work, relationships with clients and customers. The result is a team effort and a network of constructive interpersonal relationships that support the total care effort. Champy (1995) believes the first duty of leadership is to understand people's need to know—to understand where they fit into the immediate and long-term purposes of the business.

To distinguish between the responsibilities of a **nurse leader** and a **nurse manager** is to understand the focus of each (Figure 1.1). What emerges is a set of qualities or compass points that distinguish leaders from managers:

Specialists. Leaders are experts in something. Skills in coordination are not enough.

Generalists. Leaders know enough about a variety of different disciplines to be able to mediate among the specialists.

Self-Reliant. Leaders learn to think of themselves as a business of one while maintaining their value to the organization.

Connected. Leaders give up their independence and become team players. They must be good at both coordinating work teams and serving as a working member of one or more teams.

In nursing, the key factor that distinguishes leadership from management is the nurse's capacity to position and prioritize patient care with that of the organization's vision and focus on meeting patients' needs through excellence in clinical practice.

FIGURE 1.1 Differences between Leaders and Managers

LEADERSHIP	MANAGEMENT
Facilitator	Director
Coordinator	Controller
Inspiring and integrating	Telling and selling
Macromanagement	Micromanagement
Peers or followers	Subordinates
Coaching and challenging	Blaming
Problem solving and quality improvement	Problem identifying

Nurse managers are accountable for excellence in clinical practice too, but here the focus is the bottom line: with goal attainment tied to cost and rules and regulations holding sway over vision and values. Nurse managers define the playing field as it relates to care initiatives and makes clear the clinical outcomes. The best nursing units have always been the ones with the best people. It is on these units where everyone understands the business they are in: achieving excellence in patient care.

> **TIP**
>
> A critical responsibility of nursing leadership is to understand and then explain the purpose, culture, and process of excellence.

Kouzes and Posner (1990) have suggested that leaders get other people to want to do something, while managers get other people to do what they do not want to do.

> **TIP**
>
> The nurse leader determines the vision of the future, defines the path to get there, and establishes the rewards for reaching excellence in patient goals.

Leaders inspire, encourage, and serve as role models. They drive change. They are strategic. They are involved in creating new architectures of work. They are creative. And they have fun at what they do.

The leader understands there is no one right way or a perfect structure that will always succeed. Muller-Smith (1993), however, suggests that there are core skills necessary for leadership success: anticipation, resilience, and teamwork. These skills recognize the unique responsibilities of leadership and go beyond task assignment and goal achievement.

> **TIP**
>
> The true challenge for the nurse is to encourage every person to do his or her personal best.

Nurse leaders who strive to develop an environment that reinforces the value of individual contributions and considerations instill a sense of devotion and pride. They learn to be responsive to individual needs, to assess the individual goals of their staff members, and to communicate a can-do attitude.

How to Encourage High Morale and Esprit de Corps

1. Encourage positive thinking.
2. Push the status quo. Try new ideas. Find solutions. Don't say no. Take a risk.
3. Think success. Act successful. Look and be happy in your thoughts and actions. Perspective is reality.
4. Smile. A pleasant smile ignites enthusiasm and energy.
5. Be honest. Show appreciation. Say thank you. Shout praise.
6. Use a person's name when addressing him or her. A name captures attention and elicits a rapid response.
7. Act as a facilitator and integrator.
8. Change people when people will not change.

The Leadership Impact

What does it take to be a great leader? Great followers. When followers exhibit extraordinary commitment and loyalty to their leader and to their leader's vision, a shared sense of stewardship and accountability emerges.

> **TIP**
> The asset of any leader is followers. Followers are not to be commanded and controlled but understood (Champy, 1995, p. 46).

Note the vital and delicate role a leader plays. Note also the abilities and interpersonal skills that leaders must possess in order to build positive relationships with followers.

INTERPERSONAL SKILLS OF LEADERSHIP

- *Supporting and guiding.* The leader seeks to bring out the best in followers, thus creating a supportive work environment.
- *Developing and counseling.* The leader promotes personal development and satisfaction; followers aspire to achieve the goals and behaviors of the leaders, sometimes in very resource-constrained work environments.
- *Foreseeing problems.* The leader defines a mission and changes before they occur, and clarifies and assigns roles to followers. In good times and in bad, he or she helps team members to go beyond what is expected of them or even beyond what they believe they are capable of.
- *Knowing how to lift the spirits of followers.* The leader knows when to speak and when to remain silent, when to ask and when to tell, all to create and maintain the precarious leader-follower relationship.

The balancing act that leaders must perform to have an impact on job performance is tricky. The real challenge is figuring out how to keep accountability and also take full advantage of the judgment and creativity of all followers. Effective followers focus their attention first on themselves and then on the leader or the organization, or sometimes both. To ensure that followers feel trusted, respected, and challenged, the nurse leader must encourage them to try the unexplored and the untested without fear of failure. If followers are inhibited by the fear of failure, they will not dare to try. Nurse leaders can foster success through promoting a **personal best** or "give it your best shot" approach to achieving goals.

STEPS FOR PROMOTING A PERSONAL BEST AMONG FOLLOWERS

1. Encourage self-management. Foster opportunities that allow followers to think independently and work interdependently. Guide with little or no supervision.
2. Be open and forthright about the work to be done, and secure commitment. Lead with a purpose and direction in achieving tasks.

3. **Develop skill mastery.** Demonstrate the meaning behind the behaviors of a capable, competent, and confident workforce. Model and maintain high performance standards.
4. **Be courageous and credible first, and others will follow in your path.** Reward those who are risk takers, are trustworthy, and think critically.

Leaders are dependent on a capable followership because of their influence on the design, effectiveness, and quality of nursing practice. Certainly followers have an increasingly tangible and significant impact on the total organization.

> **TIP**
> Followers are responsive to the demand and drive for lower-cost care as well as the appropriate use of system resources.

Followers rely on supportive, effective leadership in which trust, integrity, and a cooperative spirit are part of the leader-follower relationship every day, on every job, in every way.

LEADERSHIP AND NURSING: A PERFECT MATCH

Leadership is a process whose essence is performance. It requires lots of work. Yet anyone who wants to work hard enough can lead. The work of leadership is both a personal and professional endeavor. Those who seek to lead effectively must possess two essential traits: empathy and expertise. Nurses possess both of these characteristics. Professional nursing views empathy as essential to caring. Clinical nursing requires empathy and expertise in management of patient care.

The foundation of effective leadership in nursing is thinking through nursing's vision clearly and visibly as it relates to the delivery of patient care. The nurse leader selects the goals, sets the priorities, and maintains standards all in support of the overriding mission of the health care organization. The effective nurse leader endeavors to understand the organization's mission and then designs a nursing mission to advance nursing practice, education, and research. She acts as the trumpet that makes the clear sound so that others may follow.

THE ROLES OF LEADERS

- **Motivators**
- **Mentors**
- **Role models**
- **Sounding boards**
- **Confessors**
- **Cheerleaders**
- **Coaches**

Leaders are responsible. When things go wrong—and they often do—leaders do not blame others but rather hold themselves ultimately responsible for the mistakes of peers and followers. Leaders see the triumphs of peers and followers as their triumphs rather than a threat.

Nurses who seek to build and sustain their energy and effectiveness as nurse leaders must evaluate their own qualities and capabilities. They must know their expertise and strengths, and, just as important, their weaknesses and how to improve them. Tagiuri (1995, p. 11) believes the following characteristics are necessary for effective leadership:

- Leaders work intensively with their subordinates when needed.
- Leaders ally themselves with subordinates in getting the job done without invading their territory and depriving them of recognition for their accomplishments.
- Leaders focus the dialogue on the work rather than on the person doing the work.
- Leaders accept a certain amount of hostility and resentment from their subordinates, an inevitable aspect of all human relationships, especially toward those with the power.
- Leaders control the human tendency to use a position of power to express hostility or anger.
- Leaders divert their subordinates' hostility and aggression away from themselves and onto the project, the challenge of the job, and the competition.
- Leaders pass on experience and knowledge and try to control their fear that a subordinate will displace them.
- Leaders help subordinates recognize and accept certain distressing but universal characteristics of work groups (e.g., struggles over authority, power, and competition for limited resources). They spend a great deal of time balancing the conflict between collaboration and

competition among subordinates and help them understand that conflict is part of life.
- Leaders carefully explain to subordinates any problems caused by their behavior, but they avoid put-downs.

To become an effective nurse leader, create a plan that builds on your existing skills and knowledge. Take the necessary steps to sharpen those skills that you already possess or compensate for the ones you lack so you can be a vital contributor. Seek to build skills that foster creative, caring leadership:

- Clarify the mission, purposes, and goals of your team.
- Describe assignments clearly.
- Listen to others' views.
- Be energetic and enthusiastic.
- Set an atmosphere where others want to achieve.
- Make clear the standards and expectations by which you will evaluate performance—what you consider important.
- Give and promote feedback on performance. Praise a good job, and offer assistance if a poor one was done.
- Merit your team's trust. Admit errors, do not lie, and if you cannot keep a commitment, explain why.

Strategies for Leading

As a nurse leader, sharpen your skills and translate them into strategies to serve those you lead:

- Say what you know clearly and directly.
- Show what you know concisely and consistently.
- Seek out information readily.
- Tell your followers you want to know the truth—the good *and* the bad.
- Hold **head-to-head meetings** or quality improvement sessions where individuals representing many functional areas gather into one room for privacy. Post a "do not disturb" sign on the door. Gently and firmly guide the followers through a series of discussions of how they would handle a range of hypothetical but plausible challenges. The goal is to think through all potential possibilities well in advance of

their happening. It may take a while for the group to be open and share ideas freely. A safe and secure environment will encourage the dialogue to occur.
- Allow followers to voice their concerns, fears, and thoughts about the evolving health care environment.
- Encourage thinking in collaborative ways by asking others for advice and help. Encourage others to give and get feedback. This feedback is vital if trust is to flourish among and between the leader and the followers. Ongoing feedback in these sessions does not replace the need for formal feedback between the leader and the follower.
- Conduct one-on-one performance reviews that encourage followers to develop and improve their skills. During this formal evaluation, point out areas of the job in which the individual is particularly accomplished and other areas that need improvement. An ongoing system of feedback benefits the individual and the organization through improved productivity and open communication.

> **TIP**
>
> If you want to interact effectively and influence others, you must seek first to understand.

Build the skills of empathic listening (Covey, 1990). Listening is the ability to understand the needs, concerns, and situations as they present themselves. If you do not listen, communication can easily become unclear, confused, and misunderstood. It is important to remember that communication goes both ways. If you truly want followers to follow, you too must follow. Listen carefully to their words and actions as they reflect all that you would like to accomplish.

Take concrete steps to ensure that all who are involved in clinical nursing understand the vision, values, and expectations as they relate to patient care delivery.

- Make the vision, values, and expectations visible by posting them in a prominent place.
- Identify daily, monthly, and quarterly goals that support and measure clinical nursing care.
- Make a progress report noting goals reached and a report card on those that need improvement.

- Make improved communication a way of linking performance to quality through frequent contact with followers. Provide for frequent contact in a variety of forums that allow followers the opportunity to act and to assess the impact of their actions and performance.

TIP

Effective communication is the link to successful performance and quality patient care.

Leaders need to keep in touch with those who are vital to the day-to-day operations of the organization—peers, followers, and other professionals. A simple way to begin each day and have immediate contact with those who report directly to you is a **stand-up meeting**. Invite at least one representative from each clinical area within your scope of leadership to make a quick status report and then field questions. Keep the meeting simple and brief—no more than 20 minutes. The purpose is to allow for face-to-face contact with early diagnosis and interventions in areas that may present problems or difficulties. After these stand-up meetings, encourage staff to develop objectives and action plans.

End each day with another contact, a **sit-down meeting** in a quiet space with the same representatives from earlier in the day and perhaps others who have experienced difficulty and seek assistance. This meeting provides a more concentrated analysis of the daily operations and responsibilities of patient care. Each attendee reports on three areas under his or her leadership that are improving and three areas that need attention. This contact provides for a status report on issues identified as most important. Followers have a public forum to share the progress of experiences and events as they relate to leadership and clinical nursing.

Encourage staff to prepare a list of specific questions on areas of concern before they attend the sit-down meeting, and ask that they take notes—not just notes of what is said during the meeting but, more important, what they will do with the information. Keeping a separate page for "to do's" will ensure that each staff member leaves with an action plan.

In between the stand-up and sit-down meetings there should be time scheduled for **please-arrange-to-see-me meetings**. A few hours of each day are set aside and divided into 15-minute segments. Any member of your staff or team can sign up in advance to discuss an idea or problem or seek advice. This open invitation creates a scheduled forum for communication to occur, not just an open-door policy of idle chatter and time wasting. By scheduling time and providing contact, you let your team know that you are accessible and approachable. There is no limit on the topic, only on the allotted time.

One final approach for keeping in contact with those you might not see daily is a very low-tech but high-yield information technique to keep the channels of communication open. Individuals are encouraged to write questions or comments on a 3- by 5-inch index card, which is then routed through the organization to someone who has the knowledge and authority to respond appropriately. As the leader of the **index-card meeting**, you are responsible for seeing that the index card makes it to the right person. When the index card receives the answer, it is returned to the original author—all within 24 hours, guaranteed.

> **TIP**
> Strong leaders establish the agenda to obtain the desired outcomes rather than wait for chaos.

The purpose behind using a variety of meeting formats is to reach out and stay in touch often and frequently. You want to see as many individuals in the organization as you can. As a leader you need to be accessible to peers, colleagues, and followers. Successful leadership is not a secret or a mystery. It simply includes being at the right place at the right time. How will you know this? Saturate the organization with communication. Trust your instincts. Play your hunches. Move around the organization and sense for yourself the problems and priorities.

> **TIP**
> Nurse leaders can have an uncanny ability to calm the waters in the face of hostility.

SUMMARY

When you trust your instincts and base your actions on principle-centered values, empathy and expertise will guide your leadership; your leadership style will promote participation and shared responsibility. It is leadership aligned on a purpose, future focused, designed to tap the creative talents of all, and filled with rewards and recognition.

As a nurse leader, you recognize the importance of creating an environment that supports staff and follower decision making. This has a profound impact on efforts to improve patient care, as well as in the design and implementation of clinical policy to support patient care systems and standards.

Rely on the voice of the nursing staff. Because of the need for follower input, strive to acknowledge and respect their values and motivations. Burns (1978) says, "Leadership is inducing followers to act for certain goals that represent the values and motivations—the wants and needs, the aspirations and expectations—of both leaders and followers" (p. 19).

The ability of nurse leaders to understand the values and motivations of those around her, as well as to listen and involve followers in decisions, benefits from a larger pool of experience. The sharing of information will result in nurse leaders' making collective changes as they shape nursing's role in the health care delivery system. This shaping and alignment of the organization over patient care, cost, and quality issues are the heart of nursing leadership.

REFERENCES

Bennis, B., and Nanus, B. (1985). *Leaders.* New York: Harper & Row.
Bolman, L. G., and Deal, T. E. (1991). *Reframing organizations: Artistry, choice, and leadership.* San Francisco: Jossey-Bass.
Burns, J. (1978). *Leadership.* New York: Harper & Row.
Champy, J. (1995). *Reengineering management.* New York: Harper Business.
Covey, S. (1990). *The seven habits of highly effective people.* New York: Simon & Schuster.
DePree, M. (1989). *Leadership is an art.* Garden City, NY: Doubleday.
Kouzes, J., and Posner, B. (1990). *The leadership challenge.* San Francisco: Jossey-Bass.
Muller-Smith, P. (1993). Beyond the basics: enhancing management skills. *Journal of Post Anesthesia Nursing, 8,* 410–412.
Tagiuri, R. (1995). Managing people. *Harvard Business Review, 72*(5), 10–11.

Chapter 2

A Shift in the Leadership Paradigm

The values of women differ very often from the values which have been made by the other sex. . . . It is the masculine values that prevail.

VIRGINIA WOOLF (1981)

The nature and complexity of health care institutions have been influenced by bureaucratic structures built on traditional, patriarchal values (Ashley, 1980; Doering, 1992). These values have operated from a Machiavellian model of power with a command-and-control style of leadership that calls for directives and orders to be passed down the chain of command from superior to subordinate. Leaders, functioning within a hierarchical structure dominated by the masculine traits of competitiveness, independence, aggressiveness, decisiveness, and self-reliance use authority and control to gain compliance, action, and results.

Leadership characterized by these traits has been defined as **traditional leadership,** or bureaucratic leaderhip, and viewed as the norm. These beliefs and perceptions have influenced organization leadership, including the use and distribution of power over the past century.

THE CHANGING NATURE OF LEADERSHIP

Pressed by global competition and a fast-changing health care system and driven by the bottom line to provide cost-effective care under capitated or preestablished budgets, nurse leaders are shifting to a new leadership style. This is a paradigm shift, from traditional, hierarchical, command-and-control structures to an innovative, nontraditional structure of sharing authority, networks, and empowered self-managed teams. This new leadership style presents a more flexible, inclusive approach—a feminine approach.

During the past decade, many changes have occurred in the health care delivery system, mostly due to market forces reacting to the shrinking health care dollar, including the dramatic shift from fee-for-service to managed care and the trend toward managed competition and integrated delivery systems (Weis, 1995, p. 23). These economic forces are influencing the redesign and reformulation of organization structures and leadership.

Survival in this time of restructuring within the health care delivery system may rest on instituting a different style of leadership—one with a new vision, a new worldview: leadership with a feminine style that acknowledges the values and voices of women. Women seek to encourage, not exclude, and they empower others, whereas men are socialized to compete as individuals and use direct control measures (Rosener, 1990).

When women's voices and leadership style influence organization structure, a different model emerges, one built on inclusion and shaped like a spider web (Borman, 1993). Helgesen (1990) views a web as a contemporary organization structure that encourages rather than commands participation in the workplace. It emphasizes collectivity and connectedness over separateness and isolation, working together in a blend of collaboration and competition, and sharing power rather than power hoarding. The following components are contained in a spider web structure:

- Networks rather than hierarchies
- Influence and persuasion over placing orders
- Organization boundaries that are flexible and permeable
- Multiple roles of leadership—teacher to learner to team member
- Invisible strands or threads of connection over chain-of-command linkages to leadership

It is time for nurse leaders, and particularly women, to abandon the patriarchal systems that lack caring, foster violence and abuse of power, and destroy and violate people's wholeness (Backer et al., 1993).

Organizational structures of health care delivery systems can be reshaped into spider webs from bureaucratic pyramids through **nontraditional leadership**—women's ways of leading (Rosener, 1992). The feminine approach or perspective is characterized by a flexible, interconnected network style that seeks to shift power away from solely those who possess a title, rank, or box in the organizational structure to everyone involved in the business of patient care.

QUALITIES OF FEMININE LEADERSHIP

- It seeks to share information and power.
- It coaches and facilitates.
- It asks questions.
- It encourages broad participation.
- It nurtures the self-esteem of others.

The feminine approach to leadership brings a new and different way of viewing the organization and its business. It creates a shift in how we think, what we identify as the most important problems, and the solutions we envision for these problems. Aburdene and Naisbitt (1992) suggest that feminine leadership is shaping the values and culture of the corporation of tomorrow.

> **TIP**
> Feminine leadership is a natural quality for nurse leaders.

Today 97 percent of all nurses are women. Women and nurses are especially adept at caring for and leading others. They are natural trust builders because they are often attuned to feelings and emotions and are aware of their surroundings. Women possess a social sense that emerges from an ethic of care. Gilligan (1982) identifies the ethic of care as "an activity of relationships, seeing and responding to the need for taking care of the world by sustaining the web of connection so that no one is left alone" (p. 62).

Nursing has always viewed human experience as surfacing from a human-environment interrelationship. Nurse leaders can extend this ethic of care in the workplace by looking to enhance other people's sense of self-worth and energizing followers. They allow others to perform their best and feel good about themselves and their work. Feminine leadership has the potential to shape the values and the culture of health care systems by humanizing the workplace through care, compassion, and empathy. Figure 2.1 lists some qualities that characterize aspects of feminine leadership.

FIGURE 2.1 Style and Characteristics of Feminine Leadership	
Power style	Contextual
	Interested in complex, more open, less defined aspects of reality
	Concerned with the total picture
	Sharing of internal resources
	Establishment of interdependent relationships
	Interest in subtleties
	Indirect
	Impression management
Negotiation style	Noncompetitive
	Emphasis on establishing, contributing to, depending on, and fostering relationships to obtain success
Achievement style	Relational
	Emphasis on relationships as means to success
	Establishing and supporting diversity
	Using collaboration and equality to obtain success
Relationship style	Involved relationship between leader and follower
	Strong commitment and involvement in the lives of followers
	Emphasis on transforming followers to higher levels of motivation, conduct, and aspirations
	Harmony achieved based on a unity that transcends differences
	Longer time perspective

FEMININE APPROACHES AND EXPECTATIONS

Command-and-control leadership is not the only way to succeed and obtain results. Although the concern for protecting the bottom line has been a driving value directing the distribution of resources in most health care organizations, it can no longer stand as the only means to achieving a goal or reaching an objective. To address the changing nature of health care institutions and the leadership style needed to guide them, I urge a contemporary feminine style that emphasizes empowerment over withholding power, collaboration over competition, and self-management over command and control.

Core Elements of Feminine Leadership

- **Wholeness**
- **Interconnectedness**
- **Equality**
- **Diversity**
- **Collaboration**

These core values are well suited to the conditions confronting nurse leaders as they deal with the constantly changing health care environment.

> **TIP**
>
> To survive and flourish within a reformed health care system, nurse leaders must value their feminine style in a system that too often devalues care, equality, diversity, and collaboration.

Feminine values will often include attention to process instead of a focus on the bottom line and a willingness to look at how an action will affect other people instead of simply asking, "What's in it for me?". "These values may be defined as female because they have been nurtured in the private, domestic sphere to which women have been restricted for so long" (Helgesen, 1990, p. xli).

To alter the devaluing of feminine qualities, beliefs, and norms in the workplace Taylor-Moss (1995) suggests using an action plan with seven strategies:

1. *Overcome hidden agendas.* Know the structures, rules, and dynamics of the organization setting; these occur in the context of a male-oriented system.
2. *Understand the existing power structure.* Stand ready to read between the lines. Most health care delivery systems are modeled after a vertical chain, top-down operation. Be familiar with the connecting lines, and know where the true power lies.
3. *Memorize the playbook.* Know the organization rules for conducting business. How is work accomplished and recognized? Are decisions made before, during, or after the meeting?
4. *Learn the corporate language.* Know the signs and symbols of organization success and failure and what they mean. Identify the sacred

cows. Listen carefully to how words are used and the context from which they are derived (e.g., the military or sports, or whether they possess a sexual flavor).
5. *Establish business and financial credibility.* Know your numbers. Financial management and analysis are critical and an essential part of health care operations.
6. *Utilize gender-specific communication styles.* Women and men have very different communication styles. Appreciate the differences and learn how to communicate effectively with both sexes.
7. *Develop political skills.* Become familiar with the politics of the workplace. Identify the strategies of influence. Be politically savvy. Use your political influence and power to obtain the necessary resources for yourself, your team members, and your patients.

When nurse leaders use a feminine approach to leadership, their voices and values focus on relationships and interdependence. Belenky, Clinchy, Goldberg, and Tarule (1989) believe women typically approach adulthood with an understanding that the care and empowerment of others is central to their life's work. Through listening and responding, they draw out the voices and minds of those they help to raise up.

Women leaders, particularly nurse leaders, use their voices as a means for both presenting themselves and what they know about the world and for eliciting a response (Helgesen, 1990). It is the voice of feminine leadership that transforms the vision into reality, and it is in this vehicle—this concern for means along with ends—that the value for connectedness grows and survives.

Feminine leadership seeks to encourage participation: getting subordinates to transform their own self-interest into the interest of the group, team, or even the organization. Nurse leaders can easily reconcile the concern for the bottom-line results with concern for people. Connected to those around them, nurse leaders do not get bogged down in giving orders but strive to inspire and direct others.

GOAL OF FEMININE LEADERSHIP

Feminine leaders strive to create an atmosphere in which people feel:

- **Confident to act on their own authority.**
- **Confident they will be supported by their leader.**
- **Confident they will not be punished for taking risks.**
- **Confident they can learn new and different responsibilities.**

Feminine leadership does not ignore the bottom line of organizational goals or objectives but seeks to value the bottom line just as much as it values the process of getting there. As nurse leaders strive to establish strategies to balance bottom-line cost issues of clinical care, they can use a feminine leadership approach to convert rigid structures into flexible boundaries, achievement, and outcome with process and involvement.

STRATEGIES FOR BALANCING SYSTEM GOALS WITH INTERPERSONAL RELATIONSHIPS

- **Share power and information. Solicit ideas and thoughts. Open communication flows in two directions. Seek to involve those most affected by the balance equation to be in the decision-making process. Encourage problem-solving processes and quality improvement programs to work out differences.**
- **Use and encourage group work over individual assignments. Pay attention to the ground rules and the expectations of each person. Be sure everyone is encouraged to participate. Allow for dissent and disagreement to be articulated and ventilated. Instill group identity, and try to make people feel part of the organization, from setting performance goals to determining strategy.**
- **Establish forums for consensus building when conflict or dissent emerges. Make it easy for people to express their ideas. Give up control, open the door to criticism, and do not be afraid to expose personal and turf conflicts.**
- **Be ready to act as a role model or mentor in bringing inclusiveness, wholeness, and balance to the workplace.**
- **Enhance the self-worth of others. Make others feel important. Give credit and praise. When someone does something out of the ordinary, send a note. Make it a point to acknowledge good work by talking about it in front of others.**
- **Energize the workplace. Show enthusiasm, and spread it around until it ignites laughter and energy. Get others excited about work. Be positive.**

TURNING REALITY ON ITS HEAD

It will not be easy to change the nature and distribution of power in traditional, bureaucratic systems of health care. The power holders will struggle against anything that challenges their control (Backer et al., 1993).

> **TIP**
>
> What counts for power, authority, and responsibility is what you can do with your skills and personal qualities (Champy, 1995, p. 22).

Feminine leadership, however, is not about taking power away; rather, it seeks a redistribution of power that allows for greater participation and equality. Feminine leadership is a key element in the reshaping of power structures and spheres of influence.

The U.S. Department of Labor reports that women make up 46 percent of the overall labor force, and 66.81 percent of all women with children under 18 are working (1991, 1992). Yet less than 5 percent of women occupy a chief executive position in hospitals (Glass ceiling, 1995). Fewer than a dozen of the 6,000 top executive officers in this country are women (Cole, 1991). And women earn approximately 70 percent of what men earn (Passell, 1992).

Nurse leaders have an obligation to identify policies that support women and make a substantial difference in their lives. It is imperative that the issues of decent pay and decent working conditions, sexual discrimination and harassment, child care and elder care, and promotion and advancement are brought to the policy table.

Helgesen (1990) notes that women do not separate their personal selves from their workplace selves, nor do they split being a mother from being a manager, being an executive from being a friend (p. 67). Women will always have one foot planted in the public sphere of the workplace and the other firmly planted in the private sphere of the home. The two are inextricably intertwined. What keeps women up at night is the reality of being assigned the major responsibility for taking care of home and family while juggling the demands of work.

Through feminine leadership, the expressed needs and concerns for women can be addressed. Women and nurse leaders must focus on women's collective strength and their ability to get what they need for themselves and their families. Why do nurse leaders need to be the voice of women? Because women are not equal yet.

The health care industry is the largest employer of women. It is here that nurse leaders can push for a safe, secure workplace that provides meaningful work with the balance of choices for merging home and work. Nurse leaders can model the way by creating a safe place to work and then transforming the workplace for others.

Working effectively within traditional, hierarchical structures requires knowing and understanding the ground rules:

1. Present a crisp, no-nonsense professional image. Physical appearance makes a difference. Be impeccable. Wear your name tag, and make sure it is clearly visible. Dress in businesslike clothing, and wear a lab coat only when it will place you in a position of strength (that is, when everyone else is wearing a lab coat).
2. Make eye contact, and use strong, direct language. Stay firm and erect. Don't allow others to interrupt your flow of thought or communication.
3. Be prepared and organized. Do your homework. When necessary, call on those whose support you will need in advance, and ask for their help.
4. Do not overuse hand gestures or movements. Quiet your body language. Too much movement will distract from what you are saying and decrease your power base.
5. Never use offensive language or off-color remarks.
6. Be honest and direct. No one knows all the answers. A simple "I don't know but will get back to you," will suffice.

CHALLENGES AND OBSTACLES

Nurse leaders who find themselves in systems that value economic efficiency over caring can turn to feminine leadership for hope, inspiration, and a new approach to leading others—one that emphasizes power sharing, group process, and consensus building. The nurse leader is well positioned to confront the resistance and reactionary scare tactics of doing business as usual. Nurse leaders must be ready to respond and demonstrate the difference that feminine approaches to leadership can make.

SKILLS AND STRATEGIES OF FEMININE LEADERSHIP

- **Promote the principles of care.**
- **Understand that each person has a center of power and wisdom within and allow that center to emerge and contribute.**
- **Listen to the voices of others, and accept them as equal to your own.**

- **Make confidence contagious.**
- **Learn to see with new eyes, and question the status quo.**
- **Redefine power as self-determination rather than domination.**
- **Develop an excitement for learning, and press professional and personal boundaries.**
- **Learn to cooperate and to appreciate and to enjoy being appreciated by others.**
- **Experience as much joy in the process as in the result.**
- **Encourage intuitive decisions as well as rational ones.**
- **Remove hierarchical structures and barriers that interfere with communication and clinical practice.**
- **Appreciate work as being a part of your life, not separate from it.**
- **Balance organizational priorities and patient needs with a human impact perspective, not just a financial one.**
- **Promote professional autonomy and growth.**

When you apply a feminine leadership approach to your practice setting, you experience a renewed sense of self and community. In this new environment that fosters collaborative, collegial relationships, struggles over issues of leadership, authority, credit, power, and participation diminish. Leaders as well as team members build an atmosphere of mutual respect, trust, and support through the development and use of process skills as well as sharing authority.

By using process skills, nurse leaders teach team members how to deal with the social forces and issues of power, conflict, change, and group dynamics. Team members develop an awareness of themselves and how they relate to others in a group. By introducing feminine principles of inclusion, connection, and responsibility to teams, nurse leaders seek to bridge the gap between the demands of efficiency fostered by most health care institutions and the need to nurture the human spirit.

Feminine principles help to reconcile a concern for bottom-line results with a concern for people. They focus on both means and ends and balance planning, directing, and communicating organizational objectives.

TIP

Using feminine principles and approaches to action reshapes leadership into a process of shared authority, empowerment, and mutual respect and trust.

Reshaping Leadership

Miller (1976) has observed that a female view of the world has valuable leadership qualities. This perspective holds that responsibility, connection, and inclusion have been devalued by our society over the rewards and recognition of the individual. Feminine leadership seeks to overcome the success of the individual for the success of the team. It seeks to end the alienation that troubles our workplaces, which push for efficiency over the need for care and compassion. Women in power and leadership positions must prove themselves to be effective. Cantor and Bernay (1992) suggest that effectiveness translates into a woman's ability to negotiate, mediate, champion causes, and compromise.

Behaviors of Feminine Leadership

- **Provide clear and concise directions.**
- **Seek accuracy in all statements and positions.**
- **Protect and maintain personal integrity.**
- **Foster positive relationships with colleagues.**
- **Secure a position on the team, and be a team player.**

By using a creative feminine leadership style to reshape and build an atmosphere that allows team members to feel accepted, respected, and supported, nurse leaders can respond creatively to team building by spinning a web and becoming more inclusive when initiating policy development and work productivity. They can be particularly effective at advocating a policy agenda based on the ethic of care because they consider both the instrumental (i.e., objective, rational) and the expressive (i.e., affective values and beliefs) components of any issue (Backer et al., 1993).

Caring in Nursing

- **A way of being that is responsive rather than judgmental or hierarchical.**
- **A range of nurturing and protective acts devoted to assessing and responding to others' needs.**
- **A belief system that encourages empowerment and emancipation for patients and team members.**

- **A way of fostering a system that comprises enabling and supportive activities.**

Helgesen (1990) suggests that integration of the feminine principles of leadership into the public sphere offers hope for healing, returning a concern for the nurturing and fostering of life to our public sphere. By reshaping leadership with a feminine approach, nurse leaders redefine and reaffirm the care and compassion needed in the public sphere of health care delivery. Given the myriad of gender differences that nurse leaders encounter every day, Heim (1995) notes some important strategies: "Play by the rules, get to the point quickly, get coaching from the boss, maintain friendliness, and get your ducks lined up before the meeting" (p. 18).

Summary

Nurse leaders have the potential to transform health care organizations into places of great care and compassion. This transformation means breaking down the barriers and values of traditional, bureaucratic leadership to nontraditional, feminine leadership. Success in health care organizations will stem from sharing power and authority, greater use of group process skills with an ear toward listening until all voices reach consensus, and more creative, flexible, integrative leadership.

References

Aburdene, P. and Naisbett, J. (1992). *Megatrends for Women.* New York: Villard Books.

Ashley, J. (1980). Power in structural misogyny: Implications for the politics of care. *Advances in Nursing Science, 2*(2), 3–22.

Backer, B., Costello-Nickitas, D., Mason, D., McBride, A., and Vance, C. (1993). Feminist perspectives on policy and politics. In D. Mason, S. Tabott, and J. Leavitt (Eds.), *Policy and politics for nurses* (pp. 18–31). Philadelphia: W. B. Saunders.

Belenky, M. F., Clinchy, B. M., Goldberg, N. R., and Tarule, J. M. (1989). *Women's ways of knowing.* New York: Basic Books.

Borman, J. (1993). Women and nurse executives. *Journal of Nursing Administration, 23*(10), 34–41.

Cantor, D. W., and Bernay, T. (1992). *Women in power.* Boston: Houghton Mifflin.

Champy, J. (1995). *Reengineering management.* New York: Harper Business.
Cole, J. (1991, May 26). Commencement speech, College of New Rochelle.
Doering, L. (1992). Power and knowledge in nursing: A feminist poststructuralist view. *Advanced Nursing Science, 14*(4), 24–33.
Glass ceiling firmly in place, panel finds. (1995, March 16). *Washington Post.*
Gilligan, C. (1982). *In a different voice: Psychological theory and women's development.* Cambridge: Harvard University Press.
Helgensen, S. (1990). *The female advantage: women's ways of leadership.* New York: Doubleday.
Heim, P. (1995). Getting beyond "she said, he said." *Journal of Nursing Administration, 19*(2), 6–18.
Miller, J. M. (1976). *Toward a new psychology of women.* Boston: Beacon Press.
Passell, P. (1992, March 25). Women's work: The pay paradox. *New York Times,* p. 2.
Rosener, J. (1990, November–December). Ways women lead. *Harvard Business Review,* 119–134.
Taylor-Moss, M. (1995). Developing glass-breaking skills. *Nursing Administration Quarterly, 19*(2), 41–71.
U.S. Department of Labor. (1991). A report on the glass ceiling initiative. Washington, DC: U.S. Government Printing Office.
Weis, D. (1995). Challenging our values: directing healthcare reform. *Nursing Policy Forum, 1*(1), 22–26.
Woolf, V. (1981). *A room of one's own.* Orlando, FL: Harcourt Brace Jovanovich.

Chapter 3

The Three P's of Leadership:
Power, Politics, and Policy

> Power is the faculty or capacity to act, the strength and potency to accomplish something. It is the vital energy to make choices and decisions. It is also the capacity to overcome deeply embedded habits and to cultivate higher, more effective, ones.
>
> STEPHEN COVEY (1990)

As a nurse leader, have you considered the importance of power, politics, and policy—the three P's—in your work? Do you want power? Are you politically savvy? Have you earned a seat at the policy table? These are critical questions to consider. Without full knowledge of how these P's fit into organization life, you will fail to influence the distribution of human and fiscal resources for patient care. Politics is inherent in any health care delivery system because health care involves multiple special interest groups competing for their piece of a limited pool of resources.

Politics is inevitable. As organizations have fewer and fewer resources, nurse leaders are forced to attend to their power and influence to secure the necessary resources for patient care and their team.

Awareness of and knowledge about power, politics, and policy are essential for providing optimal patient care in any clinical setting. Nurse leaders will need to strengthen their efforts to epitomize this principle in guiding practice outcomes and delivery of care. They must facilitate, design, and manage care delivery, focus on the coordination of care among other health providers, and create integrated networks to meet patient needs over the continuum of care.

Nurse leaders can transform health care systems to guarantee access to quality health care by developing their power bases and political skills. Grant (1995) points out that "there is no advantage in being a member of that largest group of healthcare professionals unless you apply what you know to get what you want" (p. 37).

CHAPTER 3 THE THREE P'S OF LEADERSHIP: POWER, POLITICS, AND POLICY

> **TIP**
> To use power and politics successfully, understand the workplace environment.

BECOMING POLITICAL AND POWERFUL

Nurse leaders can fashion a health care system that is caring, humane, and respectful of each individual, family, and community—as well as one that offers a full spectrum of quality services—through competence and political savvy. Menke and Ogborn (1993) define competence as technical knowledge, perseverance, problem-solving skills, and clinical acumen. Political savvy encompasses visibility, organization sensitivity, presentational skills, and good judgment.

THE BUILDING BLOCKS OF POLITICAL SAVVY

- Identify sources and uses of power.
- Develop strategies for effective political action.
- Apply the principles of power and politics to the practice of nursing leadership.
- Educate consumers, other health providers, and legislators about nursing roles in a reformed health care environment.
- Seek direct reimbursement for advanced-practice nurses.
- Design health services and systems for community-based care.
- Continue to encourage programs and policies that support health promotion and prevention.
- Realign organization relationships.
- Respond to market pressures to control costs.

Politics pertains to every aspect of life that involves some competition for the allocation of scarce resources or influencing of decision making (Costello-Nickitas and Mason, 1992 and 1993). These resources are time, money, space, people, and supplies. Menke and Ogborn (1993) define power and the use of politics as the ability to obtain, retain, and move resources. Politics also involves conflict because in any competitive struggle for resources, not everyone can emerge a victor. Those who win do so by knowing how to influence and change others' thoughts or actions.

> **TIP**
> Political knowledge is the key to handling power effectively.

Politics is built on interpersonal and collective energies. You must take the time to determine where power lies and how and with whom to forge relationships. The interpersonal side of politics requires you to read and understand others' biases, pet projects, and goals.

Political Behavior for the Workplace

- **Use the skills of persuasion and artful communication.**
- **Develop coalitions.**
- **Create meaningful interpersonal connections with those inside and outside the workplace.**
- **Understand the importance of time in developing these connections.**
- **Understand the need to appeal to the other person's needs and interests if a goal is to be reached or a resource is to be obtained.**

You cannot achieve political success without the support and assistance of others. Working collectively with others for political action can be exciting and more effective since there are more people to do the work and provide the emotional support that may be needed to sustain the political agenda (Costello-Nickitas and Mason, 1993).

The politically astute nurse leader will develop and design a support base that crosses the boundaries of professional disciplines, departments, and services. This work takes time, but it should be part of your everyday work.

Ways to Broaden Support and Work Collectively with Others

- **Greet and introduce yourself to others at every opportunity. Have a business card available to offer at each encounter.**
- **Invite associates and team members to join you for lunch.**
- **Invite colleagues from other disciplines—perhaps the new director of finance—for a cup of coffee.**

- Attend interdepartmental meetings or education programs, and be sure to share your business card with those you meet.
- Become familiar with the organization's business—its products and services—and find ways to support them.
- Let other departmental leaders know you are interested in their programs, products, and services. Ask if they could use your expertise. You never know when they may be able to help support you in the future.
- Build a support base. Work to organize and mobilize other nurse leaders to form coalitions of diverse groups within the workplace.

You must actively seek to build cooperative and collaborative relationships with others outside the nursing service. As a skillful politician, you must acknowledge the structure and function of the system in which you work. Know the chain of command, and determine the vertical and horizontal power lines.

> **TIP**
>
> Politics and power are not bad behaviors or bad words. They are essential components of leadership.

WALKING THE POWER LINE

Using power to acquire the resources you need to influence change, policy initiatives, and decisions is part of the power walk required of you. This means actively engaging in the use of power. Bennis and Nanus (1985) suggest that "power has the energy to initiate and sustain action translating intention into reality, the quality without which leaders cannot lead" (p. 15). Leadership without the appropriate use of power is not leadership at all. Be positioned to walk the lines of power.

THE POWER WALK

- Understand the traits and behaviors of a power broker.
- Know when to use traditional sources of power (e.g., reward and coercion) and nontraditional ones (e.g., empowerment and inclusion).

- Develop a positive can-do attitude.
- Become visible and sensitive to being at the right place at the right time with the right people.
- Develop the ability to get things done with others by using consensus and other joining behaviors.
- Gain control over scarce resources by knowledge, information, and facts.
- Gain access to top policymakers in the workplace by asking to be invited to meetings, receptions, and seminars.
- Establish alliances with friends and foes, team members, peers, and superiors.
- Develop cooperative and courteous interpersonal relationships.
- Use the power bases of professional nursing knowledge, experience, and expertise.

THE ART OF NEGOTIATING

Influence is a skill used to gain power in interpersonal situations. To have a positive influence with others and obtain what you want takes a winning combination.

BEING AN EFFECTIVE, INFLUENTIAL NEGOTIATOR

- Build your self-confidence.
- Ask the right questions.
- Master your selling skills.
- Develop a strong belief in your self-worth.
- Develop a good understanding of others' needs and wants.
- Develop a careful economic analysis of what you would like to obtain from the negotiations. What would you be willing to settle for? What is your bottom line?
- Negotiate with a win-win attitude. This will generally produce a more equitable result than a competitive me-against-you attitude.
- Leave the controversial issues for last. Try first to establish areas of agreement and an attitude of acceptance.
- Secure good eye contact. Look directly at your negotiating party without wavering or lowering your eyes.

- **Start with a warm smile,** even if you are about to disagree.
- **Encourage partner participation.** One of the most effective ways to have others accept your position is to have them participate in the reasoning process that leads to your point of view. Explain what your position is and why.
- **Be an attentive listener.** You may not agree with the other position, but you should never ignore it.
- **Sum up key points.** Before you leave the negotiation table, be sure everyone has a clear understanding of the agreement.
- **Be honest and fair.** If you are direct and up-front, your counterpart will do the same.
- **Do not sell yourself short.** Know your true value, and never settle for less than you want or less than you deserve.

Learning to have positive influence and negotiate a win-win outcome will help you accomplish your goals as a nurse leader. This will happen when you present an image of being politically astute and share the power of your position with others. Do team members think you can make change happen? Do team members trust you?

TIP

Define the message you want others to receive, and market that message to create the image that is needed to further your political goals.

Developing a positive image of power is important for both yourself and the profession. You can promote an image of power by a variety of means (Costello-Nickitas and Mason, 1993, p. 490).

1. Appropriate introduction of yourself through name selection, eye contact, and handshake can immediately establish you as a powerful person. If nurses introduce themselves by their first name to Dr. Smith, the physician, the nurses have set up an unequal power relationship unless the physician uses his or her first name. Not all women are socialized to initiate handshakes, but this gesture is a power strategy that is routine in male-dominated circles, including health care organizations. In Western cultures, eye contact conveys a sense of confidence and connection to the individual to whom one

is speaking. These behaviors can have a major impact on whether nurses are perceived as competent and powerful.
2. Appropriate attire can symbolize power and success. Nurses may believe that they are limited in choice of attire by uniform codes set by the hospital, but in fact the presentation of the uniform can hold the key to power. Nurse leaders need a powerful image with both team members and administrators and other professionals who are setting institutional policy. Astute nurse leaders might wear a suit rather than a uniform to work on the day of a high-level interdisciplinary committee meeting. Certainly attention to details of grooming and uniform selection can contribute to the power of staff nurses as well.
3. Conveying a positive and energetic attitude can send the message that you are a doer and someone to be sought out for involvement in important issues. Chronic complaining conveys a sense of powerlessness; the problem solver and optimist promotes a can-do attitude that suggests power and instills confidence in others.

You communicate power, influence, and authority to others through your professional image. Project the image consistent with your leadership style. Pay attention to how you speak and how you act as you speak to your team members, peers, and colleagues and superiors. As you monitor your speech and language, remember to pay close attention to your body language, which conveys more than the words you use.

Being an Image Maker

- **Stand erect and alert.**
- **Speak clearly and at an even pace. Do not rush to get your message out.**
- **Use only the necessary body movements to express your thoughts. Avoid overuse of hands.**
- **Project a favorable first impression.**

A professional image of power is founded on a strong belief in yourself. Take advantage of the opportunity to show your achievements and share the credit for success with all those who were rightfully responsible. Trust in your skills and abilities.

WORKPLACE POLITICS AND POLICY

Every workplace has its own political structure. This structure is composed of the system, players, and processes that govern the distribution of human and fiscal resources. The way to uncover and understand workplace politics and policy is to become an astute observer.

KEY ELEMENTS OF THE ORGANIZATION SYSTEM

- **Values and beliefs**
- **Philosophy**
- **Priorities and objectives**
- **Workplace climate and culture**
- **Norms and attitudes**
- **Languages, symbols, and signs**
- **Hidden agendas and unspoken rules**
- **Taboos and sacred cows**

Once you have become familiar with these key elements of the system, analyze how the structure fits into your leadership style, behavior, and actions. By conducting a systems view, you identify areas of personal sensitivity, compliance, and conflict. Without full knowledge of the system, you cannot become a principal player.

The principal players of workplace politics and policy are called **power brokers** (Costello-Nickitas, 1993). These individuals are perceived to be powerful and successful because of their ability to accomplish organization goals. Power brokers use specific and purposeful techniques and strategies.

POWER BROKER TECHNIQUES AND STRATEGIES

- **Assess who has power and determine which type.**
- **Know who gets their fair share of resources.**
- **Associate with other power brokers.**
- **Establish networks within the workplace and identify appropriate power lines.**
- **Develop an assertive and positive self-image.**
- **Maintain high visibility within the workplace.**
- **Learn the value of good eye contact.**

- **Possess the necessary knowledge and expertise to stay on the cutting edge.**
- **Maintain self-confidence and a determination to succeed.**

Power brokers know how to succeed. They are able to focus on what matters most in the workplace and to use the workplace as a learning environment. Michael (1982) believes that this success occurs from developing the following set of skills:

1. Acknowledging and sharing uncertainty.
2. Embracing error.
3. Responding to the future.
4. Becoming interpersonally competent (learning to listen, nurture, and cope with value conflicts).
5. Gaining self-knowledge.

> **TIP**
>
> Look around the workplace and identify the power brokers—those who establish the priorities, policies, and processes of the workplace.

To influence workplace practices and processes, you must attend to knowing the rules, regulations, and policies of the organization and nursing in particular.

Playing by the Organization Rules

- **Know the policies and procedures that govern nursing care and personnel.**
- **Know the formal and informal channels of communication.**
- **Know the people outside nursing services.**
- **Know the makeup of committees or task forces.**

When you know the organization rules, it becomes easier to participate in the politics of the workplace. You feel comfortable engaging in the social structure of the organization by attending social events, where you meet policymakers or power brokers in a casual setting. This connection lends itself to friendly conversation and an opportunity to share your knowledge and expertise.

Attend to listening and make mental notes of issues, problems, or items of common interest that were discussed. After the informal discussion, and if it is appropriate, send a thank-you note. Acknowledge the pleasure of this person's company, offer assistance on a particular project or policy initiative, and ask for a follow-up meeting.

How To Influence Policy

To be effective in bringing a nursing perspective to the decision-making table, carefully formulate your idea, message, and plan. Then identify the best possible means of persuasion, learn about specific motivations behind the policy issue, and seek insight from a variety of resources. These actions are essential to initiate and influence policy.

Policy can be defined as a set of principles that govern action toward a given end. The action usually has a specific purpose in mind, so as a leader your actions will often begin with a policy revision or initiative.

> **TIP**
>
> To change and influence policy, you must change situations, systems, practices, and behaviors by having your voice heard.

Lessons on Raising Your Voice

1. Seek out opportunities. Start with small unit–based and service-based activities. Then aim for the boardroom.
2. Appreciate that your bedside expertise and clinical judgment are critical factors that can be used for policy changes and initiatives.
3. Voice your concerns and ideas over issues that concern you most in the workplace (plans involving work redesign, self-directed work teams, etc.).
4. Look for places where decisions are made, and ask to be invited.
5. Develop influence with the policymakers of the organization through frequent communication and contact.
6. Let the focus of your policy activities evolve from personal interest and expertise.

7. Do your homework. Knowledge is influential.
8. Start in your own workplace, where individuals and families know and understand the difference nurses make in the health and healing process.
9. Move beyond the bedside, clinic, school, or community, to influencing policy at the level of local, state, and federal government.
10. When looking for support for your policy initiatives or changes, consider who is sympathetic but also who has the power to get it passed or implemented.
11. Make it easy for the policymaker to introduce your policy by giving him or her a prepared draft.
12. Use your grassroots networking skills to pave the way for your policy.
13. Include appropriate committee chairs in your grassroots advocacy effort.
14. Attend to the timing of events. Timing can be everything. Monitor your policy as it makes its way through the process to make sure it gets to the appropriate people at the appropriate time.
15. Work with policymakers friendly to your issue to decide beforehand what you must have and what you are willing to give away in the reconciliation process.

> **TIP**
> No one is given a seat at the policy table. You have to earn it.

The Policy Checklist

Before you can fully participate in the policy process, you must know the rules. Understand the ways and means to gain support for any policy intitatives you may have in mind. In order to influence policy development and changes, you must be fully qualified. To be qualified, you must participate and contribute to the organization's success. By understanding the organization's core processes and desired outcomes, you can earn a seat at the policy table.

Making a Policy Checklist

1. Know what you want. It is not enough to want to sit at the policy table. You need to know where you want to serve and why.
2. Know who can help and how to get to them.
3. Know how to campaign for a seat at the policy table, and build a base of support that will impress the people who make the decisions. Begin by determining:
   - Who has the power to make the appointment
   - When the decision will be made
   - What criteria will be used
   - Who might be close to the person making the appointment
   - Who else is seeking a seat at the table and what resources they have at their disposal

Once you have reviewed the **policy checklist** and are fully prepared to engage in the policy process, remember that any strategy will involve a good deal of personal work on your part. For example, if you decide that you need some support made on your behalf, you must ask for it. More than that, you must tell those whose help you are seeking to pitch for you. Be sure to follow up with those you have asked by making the telephone calls and reminding them that they have promised to support you. After the policy decision is made, tell them how it came out and thank them for their help whether you succeeded or failed.

> **TIP**
> Nurse leaders know the problems and have the solutions.

The key to advancing policy initiatives—in the workplace, the community, or the government—is in orchestrating an effective political voice.

Strategies for Advancing Policy Initiatives

- Communicate frequently through personal contact, letters, and telephone calls to policymakers.
- Take the initiative and bring your valuable expertise and perspectives to the places where policies are made.

- **Invite yourself to meetings when policy decisions will be made. If you are not invited, show up anyway and explain that you thought you could contribute.**

When you have earned a seat at the table, accept the challenge and be accountable. Stand ready to introduce your ideas into the public arena. Be prepared to present a clear message. Collect and assess your data. This information will act as a basis for delivering your influential message. Using facts and figures to support your policy initiative will demonstrate the difference nursing makes.

> **TIP**
>
> Most policy changes evolve from events or situations that have been supported by facts. This requires data collection that reflects nursing care activities from your workplace.

The best influence for initiating or changing policy is often made with a bit of luck and timing, but never without knowledge of the policy agenda, the policymakers, and the politics that are involved. Once you know them, you will be ready to move forward with a political base to promote nursing's agenda. You must be prepared to convert your policy ideas into political realities.

Turning Ideas into Political Realities

- **Begin within your own workplace by promoting collaboration, commitment, and creativity toward plans to work the system to advance your issue or cause.**
- **Recommend the appointment of nurses on key committees in the organization. Institute a professional practice committee chaired by nurses who serve as the peer review experts.**
- **Appoint nurses to the screening committee for department heads or executives to the organization.**
- **Appoint nurses to work redesign and restructuring projects.**
- **Institute strategic planning committees that include nursing's vision and voice for the future.**

Summary

For nurse leaders, politics is a critical element in understanding, planning, and executing nursing resources. Use power and politics to advance nursing's vision and goals in the workplace. Do not waste energy and remain powerless. Rather, learn the art and skill of political maneuvers. (You can never be skilled enough in the art of politics.)

If you are to improve the quality of nursing practice, become involved in the three P's of leadership. Accept that the health care delivery system is part of the political world. To participate fully in this world, you must understand the element of strategy involved in political action, including understanding, studying, and applying the internal moves that allow you to maintain or develop power.

President Kennedy called politics a "noble undertaking" because it is an attempt to develop policies that ennoble society by strengthening democracy. As a nurse leader, you have the expertise and experience to influence health care policies, practice policies, and workplace policies. You have to look into yourself to discover how that power and knowledge should be used.

References

Bennis, W., and Nannus, B. (1985). *Leaders.* New York: Harper & Row.
Costello-Nickitas, D. M. (1993). Making a case for nursing: Earning a seat at the policy table. *Revolution—The Journal of Nurse Empowerment, 2*(2), 58–60, 94.
Costello-Nickitas, D. M., and Mason, D. J. (1992). Power and politics in the health care organization. In P. Decker and E. Sulliven (Eds.), *Nursing administration: A micro/macro approach for effective nurse executives* (pp. 45–67). Norwalk, CT: Appleton & Lange.
Costello-Nickitas, D. M., and Mason, D. J. (1993). Power and politics. In P. Decker, and E. Sullivan (Eds.), *Effective management in nursing* (pp. 483–493). Norwalk. CT: Appleton & Lange.
Covey, S. (1990). *Principle-centered leadership.* New York: Simon & Schuster.
Grant, A. (1995). Flex your muscle. *Canadian Nurse, 91*(3), 37–41.
Menke, K., and Ogborn, S. E. (1993). Politics and the nurse manager. *Nursing Management, 24*(12), 35–37.
Michael. D. (1982). Planning and learning from it. In Jo Richardson (Ed.), *Making it happen* (pp. 175–180). Washington, DC: U.S. Association for the Club of Rome.

Chapter 4

Expanding the Power Universe

People must know that their ideas will be listened to and, if they have merit, acted upon.

JAMES CHAMPY (1995)

As organizational restructuring and work redesign take hold within the health care delivery system, shifts in power within the workplace will raise questions as to how nurse leaders will develop and use power. Creating environments in which nurses feel and act empowered will contribute to promoting high-quality patient care. The freedom to make patient care decisions and to control professional practice is critical to empowerment. After all, it is the professional nurse whom the patients know, the one they turn to, and the one they hold accountable for their care. It is imperative that nurse leaders understand this professional nurse–patient relationship and begin the process of guiding and directing power from a command-and-control leadership to empowerment of the individual and team members, thus fostering greater accountability.

> **TIP**
>
> Empowering team members is challenging. The assumption of responsibility and accountability cannot be forced; it takes time to adjust. And not everyone wants to be empowered.

A Shared Responsibility

Empowered nurse leaders shape how care is delivered. Nurse leaders clearly understand that doing business as usual with regard to patient care delivery cannot continue. New approaches are required, and they will involve a total organizational effort and commitment to changing the way health care is delivered (Sovie, 1992).

To meet the challenges of a changing health care system as well as demands for lower costs while maintaining quality, nurse leaders can effectively respond by implementing a **collaborative leadership** approach in which team members have a role and a voice in patient care decisions. This shared responsibility encourages and energizes team members who want to work together to achieve high-quality outcomes. By actively supporting those who provide the direct care, nurse leaders build both efficiency and morale.

To transform health care systems into places where nurses feel connected between self and others, are encouraged to promote their clinical expertise, and accept the challenge to restructure the workplace, nurse leaders must embrace the concept of **empowerment**: "a process of enhancing feelings of self-efficacy among organizational members through the identification of conditions that foster powerlessness and through their removal by both formal organizational practices and informal techniques of providing efficacy information" (Conger & Kanungo, 1991, p. 474).

> **TIP**
>
> Foster empowerment by encouraging team members to use their knowledge and talents creatively to improve clinical care and the workplace environment. Remind team members of their authority to make decisions about interventions and activities that take place as part of their daily practice.

From Power to Empowerment

Empowerment means giving people their own power, not yours (Jeffries, 1992). It involves enabling others to recognize and feel their strengths, abilities, and personal power. The essence of empowerment is increasing the behavior potential of persons, individually and within teams and organizations. Putman (1991) defines behavior potential as the "totality of behaviors that are actually available to a given person in a given environment. . . . Behavior potential is the intersection of the person's behavioral productions with the organization's expectations and permissions. An individual is empowered to the extent she possesses a rich repertoire of behaviors and is expected and permitted to make full use of this repertoire by the organization" (p. 4).

Wheeler and Chinn (1989) note that "empowerment requires listening inwardly to our own senses as well as listening intently and actively to others, consciously taking in and forming strength" (p. 2). Gibson (1991) suggests that empowerment be viewed as a social process of recognizing, promoting, and enhancing people's abilities to meet their own needs, solve their own problems, and mobilize the necessary resources in order to feel in control of their own lives.

Empowerment can be demonstrated through increased problem-solving abilities, improved communication, increased satisfaction with work, and increased self-esteem, autonomy, and responsibility (Hawks, 1992, p. 611). Empowerment helps individuals rise to a level of maturity where they will make the right and reasonable decision (Champy, 1995, p. 25).

> **TIP**
>
> In order to facilitate empowerment, nurse leaders must examine the philosophy underlying its practice and be prepared to educate, advocate, and effect changes that are consistent with the notion of empowerment.

It is time for nurse leaders to move beyond the traditional sources of power to empowerment. Power by coercion and force with limited access to decision making are barriers to nurses' empowerment. Therefore, if nurse leaders are to subscribe to breaking down the barriers of control, coercion, and force with empowerment, they need to legitimize the beliefs that team members are equal partners in the health care team. For the empowerment process to take hold, nurse leaders must assume the roles of facilitator and resource person as opposed to the roles of telling and selling found in supervision. Nurse leaders need to develop a commitment to serve rather than accumulate power for personal use.

ATTRIBUTES THAT BUILD EMPOWERMENT

- **Courage**
- **Commitment**
- **Intuitive understanding**
- **Flexibility**
- **An appreciation of diversity**
- **Tolerance**

- **Compromise**
- **Empathy**

Nurse leaders have a responsibility to provide the necessary support, information, and opportunities that will successfully empower team members (Chandler, 1991).

Health care systems must shift from believing in the efficacy of a hierarchical, command-and-control organization to systems that are more responsive to an empowerment model. This includes making a deliberate choice—

the choice to accept personal accountability for one's decisions; the choice to support the clinical or managerial expertise of one's colleagues; the choice to respect cultural diversity among nurses; the choice to honor patients' decision about care; the choice to accept the challenge of transforming the work environment through collaboration among nurses, other health care providers, and administrators. (Holly, Millor, and Skelly, 1994, p. 2)

Empowerment means many things to many people, but for nurse leaders, it is an act of building, developing, and increasing power through cooperating and working together. Empowerment cannot occur in a vacuum. It requires involvement at every step of the way—from identifying problems to analyzing them to proposing and implementing solutions.

Nurse leaders can promote a greater understanding of empowerment in the workplace by promoting the professional development of team members.

How to Promote Professional Development

- **Encourage the freedom and autonomy to practice professional nursing.**
- **Encourage and promote greater accountability.**
- **Build confidence and trust in decision making (Backer, Costello-Nickitas, and Mason-Adler, 1994).**

Despite attempts to move beyond power to empowerment, some people will reject it or seek to impede it. They may fear letting go, loss of control, misplaced trust, betrayal, loss of popularity, and failure (Champy, 1995).

Empowerment is a whole new ideology, a new way of thinking about power. It requires nurse leaders to shift away from power over, as in the chains of command and the lines of authority, to the sharing of information and power openly and freely.

Most health care systems by their very nature are highly bureaucratic and controlled. Often nurse leaders are exposed to the bureaucracy as a barrier to empowerment through the following ways:

- Attempts to maintain the status quo.
- Concerns of task achievements and cost savings over quality.
- Unequal distribution of power.
- Fostering **horizontal violence**, which "refers to intergroup conflict among people in the same stratum in the hierarchy. It includes intolerance of differences and unequal power relationships" (Backer, Costello-Nickitas, and Mason-Adler, 1994, p. 6).

To counteract forces of horizontal violence and bureaucracy, nurse leaders can seek a positive approach to intergroup conflict through:

- Facilitating collaboration over competition.
- Encouraging the development of a sense of community over individualism and connectedness over isolation.

The Empowerment Model

Nurse leaders must take the responsibility to begin to break down the barriers of empowerment and model the way. Leadership and managerial support of empowerment are critical if nurses are to experience empowerment in the workplace. One way is to use a **shared governance model** that promotes and supports decentralized power sharing and decision making. Within this model, team members participate and determine their own future. Shared governance allows for critical and ongoing strategic and work-restructuring decisions to occur at the point of direct patient care. When team members are encouraged to design, determine, and commit to ownership of patient services, empowerment becomes a workplace reality.

Empowerment Model Goals

- **Share information.**
- **Listen actively.**

- **Encourage risk taking.**
- **Provide for a nurturing, caring environment.**
- **Create self-directed teams.**
- **Break down barriers and encourage greater flexibility.**
- **Push for greater tolerance.**
- **Appreciate diversity.**
- **Move cooperativeness to collectivity.**
- **Allow for intuitive understanding as well as rational, logical thinking.**
- **Encourage empathy and compassion.**

If team members are to subscribe to an empowerment model, they need to legitimize the belief that they are seen as equal partners on the health care team. When they fully engage in the empowerment process, they are able to assert control over the factors that affect their professional responsibilities.

A fully empowered team offers a number of benefits: personal fulfillment, self-efficacy, a sense of mastery, a sense of control, and a sense of connectedness. By supporting a movement toward empowerment, power sharing, and feminine approaches to leadership, nurse leaders can restructure the health care environment to become more inclusive, humanistic, and caring. And by modeling empowerment behaviors, they encourage and promote empowerment in team members, patients, and others.

> **TIP**
>
> In order to subscribe to an empowerment model, nurse leaders must examine the philosophy underlying its principles and practice and be prepared to advocate, educate, and effect changes that are consistent with the values of empowerment.

When nurse leaders are prepared to share their knowledge and expertise and demonstrate a commitment toward and respect for diversity, the groundwork is laid for empowerment to take hold. The power to act according to your own values instead of being acted upon by other people and events is empowerment. Nurse leaders have the choice to promote harmony, balance, and integration among team members in the workplace by letting go of the command-and-control style of leadership.

Learning to Surrender Control

Nurse leaders must provide support and training in empowerment by educating team members to take action on behalf of themselves and their patients (Mason and Costello-Nickitas, 1990). To enable team members to feel comfortable with the concepts of empowerment and to develop the skills and approaches needed to enhance their power and influence in the workplace, nurse leaders must be committed to the notion of sharing control.

Sharing Control

- **Understanding how traditional sources of power are used and abused.**
- **Understanding how to use power to gain and share resources.**
- **Understanding that power and empowerment are active processes.**
- **Understanding that empowerment is part of a collective decision making.**
- **Understanding that developing a support base of networks, coalitions, and power brokers is a requirement of sharing control.**
- **Understanding that empowerment builds self-reliance and self-efficacy.**

To promote an equitable distribution of power in the workplace Mason, Backer, and Georges (1991) suggest using empowerment as a model for political action. This model seeks to develop three dimensions:

1. Raising the consciousness of the sociopolitical realities of a nurse's world.
2. Building strong and positive self-esteem.
3. Using political skill to negotiate and change the health care system.

A prerequisite to surrendering control to others through empowerment is a personal plan to unify and commit yourself and to develop politically astute skills for change. This sense of commitment begins by improving your self-concept and self-esteem. As a nurse leader, you must learn to use power strategies on your own behalf and then for your patients and team members.

As you acknowledge and appreciate your own abilities and strength and share these with others, you make a commitment to empowerment. Empowerment mobilizes your resources and enables change in constructive and creative ways. It involves enabling others to recognize their talents and contributions in the workplace as well as experiencing a sense of personal power.

> **TIP**
>
> To be empowered is to experience a sense of hope, excitement, and energy (Costello-Nickitas and Mason, 1992).

CREATING SELF-DIRECTED TEAMS

Begin the process of empowerment by creating **self-directed teams** that use collective decision making. Wellins, Byham, and Wilson (1991) describe self-directed teams as

> *an interactive group of employees who are responsible for a whole work process or segments that delivers a product or service to an internal or external customer . . . people who normally work together on an ongoing day to day basis. (p. 3)*

Start by encouraging team members to decide for themselves the standards and quality of clinical goals.

Self-directed teams are capable of making and implementing decisions, and they are held accountable for the results. Allow the empowerment process to transform the way team members identify and confront patient or workplace issues.

STRATEGIES FOR CREATING SELF-DIRECTED TEAMS

1. Involve every team member at every level and function.
2. Get team members to articulate specific and concrete ideas. As you think about how best to prioritize the ideas, be sure to encourage team members to link these ideas to the workplace vision.
3. Provide the team with questions to facilitate brainstorming:
   - What are the critical patient care issues facing the team and/or organization?

- How can the team use the vision to resolve these issues?
- How can we facilitate each team member's commitment and contribution to these issues?
- How can we take ownership and decide how the issues should be resolved through the empowerment process?

4. Encourage team members to take calculated risks. Confident that you, the nurse leader, will support them when unfamiliar with a situation, team members will feel free to seek your advice with no loss of self-esteem or self-doubt.
5. Establish circles of support and create a coaching mechanism whereby team members strive to develop their personal power. By learning to coach each other, team members feel secure to undertake more or different challenges and suitable initiatives on their own authority.

> **TIP**
>
> Empowerment puts the authority and decision making into the hands of team members, where it has to be.

Montisano-Marchi (1990) suggests that properly applied empowerment activities are a means for developing self-discipline along with mutual confidence. In self-directed teams, members become reliant on diffused horizontal power, concerned with the sharing of resources, collective problem solving, and the development of interdependent and cooperative relationships. Shared resources and cooperative relationships balance the power scale between leading and following, as the situation demands.

COLLECTIVE DECISION MAKING

The **collective decision-making process** is an important component of self-directedness. Although it is time-consuming, it is valued for its ability to generate creative solutions for problem solving. In this democratic process, team members are more likely to favor and abide by the outcomes because they represent their interests and concerns.

Shared decision making is best known for its ability to produce decisions that represent the broadest interests and often involve those who have most at stake. By encouraging team members to engage in dialogue and listen to the responses of others prior to making a final decision, nurse leaders build colleagueship. Carlson-Catalano (1992) suggests that collegiality is a strategy that allows nurses to call on each other for counsel regarding clinical and professional problems, thereby developing a knowledge and support network. Sharing information, support, and resources promotes social cohesion and cooperation, all necessary for effective decision making.

One way that collective decision making can lead to improved patient care and colleagueship is through a work restructuring process. As health care institutions seek to redefine themselves in a managed care marketplace, nurse leaders can be positioned to empower team members through a work restructuring process of evaluating and redefining their roles in patient care delivery.

WORK RESTRUCTURING

1. Foster a collaborative team-oriented environment in which members are committed to the concept of restructuring.
2. Establish a direction of what the guiding principles and goals of a restructuring process will entail.
3. Ask team members to identify patient needs and work flow requirements.
4. Ask team members to determine what tasks may be delegated safely, what functions can be decentralized, and what functions are truly within the domain of nursing.
5. Ask team members to evaluate patient mix, acuity, and requirements.
6. Encourage and enable team members to determine what is necessary from other departments within the organization.
7. Ask team members to describe and define the resources needed for patient care requirements and how much they will cost.

Work restructuring provides team members an opportunity to realign their roles efficiently and effectively. As teams become empowered and more self-directed, they are sensitized to the personal needs and feelings of other team members. Faith and trust in others' judgment, expertise, and competence begin to emerge as power and responsibilities are shared. Team members learn to recognize feelings of fear, despair, and confusion as they become self-disciplined. This allows trust to flourish along with nurturance and support to develop among team members.

> **TIP**
>
> By creating and encouraging self-directed teams through work restructuring and empowerment, you are giving team members the opportunity to expand their own power.

Nurse leaders who encourage and enable team members to master their workplace environment and achieve self-determination must lead the way by:

- Coordinating staffing, scheduling, and performance standards.
- Integrating patient care priorities with organizational resources.
- Facilitating human, fiscal, material support, and systems resources.
- Initiating decision-making forums for issues that support clinical practice.
- Communicating expectations.
- Providing ongoing education, training, and development.
- Delegating.
- Holding team members accountable.
- Following up through feedback and coaching.
- Acknowledging performance and rewarding successes.

Tannenbaum (1954) has described five behavioral tasks for leaders that facilitate the process of empowerment:

1. *Create situations conducive to learning.* By defining the work as a learning situation, nurse leaders underscore the developmental aspect of empowerment. The nurse leader's role is to establish the necessary learning climate.
2. *Establish a model of behavior.* Nurse leaders' willingness to take risks, change work patterns, recognize their own strengths and limitations, and actively integrate self and work provide others with the models for trying out empowerment.
3. *Introduce new values.* Empowered nurse leaders implicitly or explicitly introduce new values that encourage empowerment to happen. Accepting the validity of value clarification and allowing time for that process to take hold is important to the implementation of an empowerment model in the workplace.
4. *Facilitate the flow of communication.* Empowerment requires information sharing, especially as it relates to expectations of group process, team building, and self-directed work.

5. *Participate as an expert.* Nurse leaders' key function is to allow team members to become empowered themselves. They begin this process by sharing their expertise developed from professional experience, research, and education. Knowing when to be expert is a critical factor in the empowering process. Too much expertise increases dependency and reduces empowered behavior; however, sharing expertise to eliminate unhealthy blockages can empower team members to move forward.

> **TIP**
>
> Empowerment implies accountability. Team members must accept responsibility for what they do.

Jeffries (1992) believes that leaders must enable followers to find their vision and develop their mission statement. This is fundamental to empowering and helping followers to do their best work. As a nurse leader, you must foster a workplace climate and culture that supports, values, and facilitates the best choices and actions by team members.

Kanter (1977) suggests that individuals who are in positions that give them access to crucial resources of information, support, supplies, relevant job activities, and opportunity for advancement are more likely to exhibit empowered behaviors.

> **TIP**
>
> Empowerment is a process that requires knowledge, information, competencies, skills, resources, opportunities, and results, all of which must be fostered and facilitated by nurse leaders.

The capacity for effective action is an essential component of any meaningful conceptualization of empowerment (Staples, 1990).

When the necessary resources are placed into the hands of team members, they feel empowered. Energize them, and foster an environment that encourages creative thinking (Leob, 1995). Inspire risk-taking behaviors and push for achievement orientation and higher career aspirations. Only through this active effort of moving empowerment through the culture of the organization will positive results be produced.

KEY BEHAVIORS OF EMPOWERMENT

1. Motivation is an individual matter. As a nurse leader, rethink your strategies for motivating your team members. Consider their unique personal and developmental circumstances. This personal attention heightens the importance of your relationship with each team member.
2. The human condition is to grow and excel. Challenge team members to create career plans, and help them reach their full potential. Recharge their professional batteries by suggesting journal readings, research reports, and educational training programs.
3. Human motivation is a multidimensional experience with multiple levels of responsibility.
    - The *individual* is responsible for envisioning the future and all the possibilities life has to offer.
    - The *nurse leader* is responsible for recognizing each team member's learning style, asking, listening, challenging, and fostering growth.
    - The *organization* is responsible for designing and implementing policies that energize, motivate, and demonstrate a commitment to empowerment.

Vogt and Murrell (1990) suggest that there is a chain of relationships between the employee, the leader, and the organization and the effect of policies and strategies on the principal framework for empowerment. These relationships can foster an individual's sense of well-being and support his or her life experiences. Therefore, empowerment starts with self but does not stop there. The experience of being with others and sharing common concerns can engender strength and hope. Alternate explanations, new options, and solutions for change can be revealed. Self-directed teams help to remove the isolation of private misfortune and replace it with a new sense of self-confidence and potency. It is through the process of increased and shared participation that team members experience empowerment. Power affiliated with a purpose rejects the splintering and isolation of others.

TIP

Empowerment charges and energizes the relationship among tasks, challenges, achievements, and feelings of connectedness.

Nurse leaders determine and facilitate an entrepreneurial spirit and climate of empowerment. Jacob (1995) believes a climate of innovation and creativity will encourage productivity in individuals and teams. With encouragement and strong support from nurse leaders and the organization, team members are empowered, strengthened, and enriched to contribute and make a difference.

The key that holds empowerment together is compassionate leadership (Dobbs, 1993). **Compassionate leadership** is characterized by openness, receptivity to ideas, caring, dignity, and respect toward others. Compassionate leadership acknowledges that a nurse leader's role is to pave the way, breaking down barriers and building hopes.

SUMMARY

Empowerment can be the key that unlocks the barriers to the restructuring of health care systems. Nurse leaders have the potential to create a path to improving the quality of health care delivery by encouraging and facilitating empowerment in the workplace. To create this transformation to quality and empowerment, nurse leaders must begin by sharing information and power with those they supervise and learn the skills and strategies of a feminine approach to leadership.

To change the workplace environment radically and foster an environment in which team members have the information, power, and authority they need to make things happen, nurse leaders must build an empowerment model. This includes defining, educating, and training team members to become empowered.

A true empowered environment is egalitarian, open, and team driven or self-directed. Because empowerment requires a fundamental cultural transformation, it is a long and difficult journey. There may be some resistance along the way, but that should not dissuade anyone from the process of providing ongoing direction and encouragement. Sharing information and power, promoting collective decision making, and creating self-directed teams are the wave of the future. Empowerment is beyond power. It is an energy force that begins within one's self and goes beyond the universe.

REFERENCES

Backer, B. J., Costello-Nickitas, D. M., and Mason-Adler, M. (1994). Nurses' experience of empowerment in the workplace. *Journal of the New York State Nurses Association, 25*(2), 4–7.

Carlson-Catalano, J. (1992). Empowering nurses for professional nursing practice. *Nursing Outlook, 40*(3), 139–142.

Champy, J. (1995). *Reengineering management.* New York: Harper Business.
Chandler, G. (1991). Creating an environment to empower nurses. *Nursing Management, 22*(8), 20–23.
Conger, J., and Kanungo, R. (1991). The empowerment process: Integrating theory and practice. *Academy of Management Review, 13*(3), 471–482.
Costello-Nickitas, D. M., and Mason, D. J. (1992). Power and politics in the health care organization. In P. Decker and E. Sullivan (Eds.), *Nursing administration: A micro/macro approach for effective nurse executives.* Norwalk, CT: Appleton & Lange.
Dobbs, J. (1993, February). The empowerment environment. *Training and Development,* 44–55.
Gibson, C. H. (1991). A concept analysis of empowerment. *Journal of Advanced Nursing, 16*(13), 354–361.
Hawks, J. H. (1992). Empowerment in nursing education: Concept analysis and application to philosophy, learning and instruction. *Journal of Advanced Nursing, 17,* 609–618.
Holly, C., Millor, G., and Skelly, A. (1994). Empowering environments for caring. *Journal of the New York State Nurses Association, 25*(2), 3.
Jacob, R. (1995). Corporate reputations. *Fortune, 131*(4), 54–64.
Jeffries, E. (1992). *The heart of leadership: Influencing by design.* Dubuque, IA: Kendall/Hunt Publishing Co.
Kanter, R. M. (1977). *Men and women of the corporation.* New York: Basic Books.
Leob, M. (1995). Ten commandments of managing creative people. *Fortune, 131*(1), 135–136.
Mason, D. J., Backer, B.J., and Georges, C. A. (1991). Toward a feminist model for the political empowerment of nurses. *Image: Journal of Nursing Scholarship, 23*(2), 72–77.
Mason, D. J., and Costello-Nickitas, D. M. (1990). Empowering nurses for politically astute change in the workplace. *Journal of Continuing Education in Nursing, 22*(1), 5–10.
Montisano-Marchi, N. (1990). Power: From commanding turf to generating excellence. *Nursing Management, 21*(11), 72b–72f.
Putman, A. (1991). Empowerment: In search of a viable paradigm. *Performance Improvement Quarterly, 4*(4), 4–11.
Sovie, M. (1992). Care and service teams: A new imperative. *Nursing Economics, 10*(2), 94–100, 125.
Staples, L. (1990). Powerful ideas about empowerment. *Administration in Social Work, 14*(2), 29–43.
Tannenbaum, R., Kallajian, V., and Weschler, I. R. (1954). Training managers for leadership. *Personnel, 30,* 3–11.
Vogt, J., and Murrell, K. (1990). *Empowerment in organizations: How to spark exceptional performance.* San Diego, CA: Pfeiffer and Co.
Wellins, R. S., Byham, W. C., and Wilson, J. M. (1991). *Empowered teams.* San Francisco: Jossey-Bass.
Wheeler, C. E., and Chin, P. L. (1989). *Peace and power: A handbook of feminist process* (2d. ed.). New York: National League for Nursing.

Chapter 5

Teamwork: A Leader's Solution

Gettin' good players is easy. Gettin' 'em to play together is the hard part.
CASEY STENGEL (1992)

Teams are essential, and managing them is a natural component of leadership. No one person has all the answers. Today's health care environment is complex, and most problems require more than a simple solution or set of individual skills to solve them.

> **TIP**
>
> To solve quality problems in the health care delivery system, all those involved with caregiving must successfully work together.

The time is ripe for intra- and interdisciplinary teamwork. No one person can make all the improvements in health care. The effects of cost containment, shortened lengths of stay in acute care, expanded use of technology, and society's shifting values of doing more with less require a multiteam effort. Teamwork is a solution no leader can do without.

WHY TEAMWORK?

Understanding how teams work effectively and productively can facilitate both the leader's and the team's performance. It is ultimately the successful performance of each team that measures its effectiveness. In nursing, **team effectiveness** can be measured by creating and maintaining excellence in the clinical care of patients. How effective is your team in achieving excellence in care? Do your criteria for excellence go beyond quantitative measures of budgeting, staffing, compliance, recruitment, and education? Have you considered other quality indicators that reflect a consumer perspective of patient-centered care?

COMPONENTS OF PATIENT-CENTERED CARE

- Team members are responsive to patient needs.
- Team members demonstrate a willingness to serve.
- Team members are reliable, dependable, accurate, and trustworthy.
- Team members uphold a patient's request for confidentiality.
- Team members display empathy through caring.
- Team members provide for individualized attention.

The effectiveness of a team also depends on the contributions made by the leader. Each leader must challenge and commit team members to a common purpose, a common set of performance goals, and a common ground for which they hold themselves mutually accountable. To create and build an effective team, leaders must implement strategies that move team members to these common components.

> **TIP**
> So much of what a leader says and does affects the efforts of the team.

HOW TO ESTABLISH EFFECTIVE NURSING TEAMS

1. Define the critical nursing processes and establish complementary objectives. Teams need to focus on a limited number of core processes that contribute to achieving quality patient care.
2. Apply the 80/20 rule in problem solving: 80 percent of your success comes from 20 percent of what you do. Do the crucial things first and best. Identify and fix a few key conditions that will achieve the majority of the goals you have set.
3. Learn through benchmarking. To avoid the reinventing-the-wheel syndrome in problem solving, teams should take the time to identify and incorporate selected patient care practices that

have been demonstrated to be successful from other nursing units or organizations.
4. **Leverage information technology.** Teams should plan to draw on nursing informatics to diagnosis and problem solve.
5. **Invest adequate resources in the teamwork effort.** If you expect to use teams to solve problems and use a results-oriented approach to patient care, provide the necessary support: technology, people, money, and time.
6. **Use models or exercises to drive home the importance of teamwork.** Show and demonstrate how individuals can work together better as a team. It is one thing to teach the skills and another to show team members how to incorporate the skill into everyday work life.
7. **Pilot and monitor teamwork.** Allocate your managerial time and attention to team development. This is a terrific way to put a positive spin on teamwork and move forward in improving the development process.

Nurse leaders must seek to create an environment that supports quality management and fosters highly functional teamwork. Remove the barriers that prevent or obstruct good team performance: inadequate resources, poor equipment, and dysfunctional team players.

TECHNIQUES TO KEEP THE TEAM ROLLING

- **Coach and counsel individual team members** about their special expertise and why they are vital to the team.
- **Coach team members on process.** Listen to their explanations of the problems, and coach on how team members can and do work together.
- **Coach and assist team members to become aware of each other's struggles and conflicts.** Suggest ways in which team members can create a safety or buffer zone to say: "Hey! Pay attention to me. It's not going well, and I need help."
- **Create a network of social support.** Contact a neutral party outside the unit or department who can counsel team members or the whole team when the need arises.
- **Encourage and support the team** so that members are trained properly to do their work.

Learning to direct and manage a team requires nurse leaders to lead with less positional power and more from sharing of power and information, listening more and telling less. Learning to deploy and use people differently is vital.

> **TIP**
>
> By granting teams the power to find the solutions and create the results, nurse leaders enable teams to develop a common language and common set of goals (Meyer, 1994).

To keep the team rolling and on track, Peters (1994) suggests that leaders master:

- A bias for action
- A thirst for learning and homework
- A willingness to confront ambiguity
- A passion for success
- A willingness to shoot straight
- A penchant for revolution
- A love of laughter

By mastering these activities for keeping a team on track, nurse leaders create a desirable or ideal state to implement their goals. While goal attainment is vital, nurse leaders must define their vision.

THE VISION

Defining the Vision

To define a vision, consider your ideas, thoughts, and focus on patient care, nursing, and health care. In which direction will you lead the team? These questions need to be asked if you are going to initiate and sustain your ideas, thoughts, and focus into reality. Identify a situation in which you desire greater teamwork and synergy. What conditions would you need to support and implement your vision? What do you need to create those conditions? By translating your vision to what you are striving for and by defining goals or objectives, you should be able to have a clear idea of a future desired state. According to Block (1988), this is the definition of a **vision:** a preferred future, a desirable or ideal state. It is an expression of hope.

To create a vision Jeffries (1992) suggests letting the vision speak inside you; it should come from your heart, not your head. A vision often embodies an ideal that is value directed and future oriented. It generates energy and excitement. Translating the vision into action requires courage, commitment, and conviction. Bennis and Nanus (1985) describe leaders who are able to acquire and wear their visions like clothes. These leaders translate their beliefs into action. This process of translation means that as the team leader, you are responsible not only for creating the vision but for delineating, communicating, and evaluating it.

Creating a Vision

To create a vision is simply to express your hopes or desires. It may involve the desire to find solutions to underlying problems or to change your dissatisfaction with the current state of affairs.

How to Create a Vision

1. Draft your vision as one sentence or paragraph. Keep it simple.
2. Share your vision.
3. Seek insights from mentors as you move your vision forward. But remember that only you have the capacity to hold the vision.
4. Introduce your vision. Let your team see it. Post it in the nursing conference room or office on a flip chart.
5. Let others respond to this new journey, and invite them to come along.

No vision is worth having if it cannot be shared, transformed, and acted upon. Remember that the vision becomes the purpose of teamwork—the framework around which the values, priorities, and goals are developed. Individual and team commitment are gained by encouraging participation in how the vision is moved into action.

> **TIP**
>
> Create a vision, and make it clear. Clear visions have a positive effect on the unit, the organization, and the team. They provide a structure for goal achievement and guide directions (Gregory, 1995).

Moving the Vision to Action

Managing a team with a specific vision, such as to provide quality nursing care, can be difficult. Team leaders are responsible for assessing and identifying each member's strengths and weaknesses. They must coordinate the team's attributes to get the work done as efficiently as possible. Holladay and Coombs (1993) suggest a strong delivery style (increased eye contact, use of gestures and facial expression, increased vocal variety, and verbal fluency) for sharing and moving the vision into action.

TEAM LEADERSHIP

Team leaders need an eye for detail, a bias for action, and strong organizational skills. They use patience, insight, and diplomacy with consistency and fairness and provide a sound foundation for teams to grow and flourish. These team leadership qualities are important for nurse leaders who are building or redesigning a team.

QUALITIES FOR BUILDING OR REDESIGNING A HIGH-PERFORMANCE TEAM

1. **Vision.** Create a vision that gives the team a focus.
2. **Mission.** Provide a mission, or purpose, that motivates.
3. **Common goals.** Agree on a purpose, commit to action, and assume accountability.
4. **Mastery of role and responsibility.** Provide a clear sense of role expectation, ensure competency in required skills, and provide for constant training and development.
5. **Communication.** Build relationships on openness. Find ways to manage conflict and differences while maintaining team members' self-esteem.

6. **Intimacy, trust, and subtlety.** Create a climate of patience and clarification, go for simplicity, and reward assertiveness.
7. **Commitment.** Reinforce and celebrate when the vision is accomplished. Comment on how people are doing things right.
8. **Strive for excellence.** Work toward continuous improvement. Set standards, measure progress, and fix the problem, not the blame.
9. **Have fun.** Work hard but know when to play. Support each other in the good times and the bad.

Team leaders should define which core qualities are most important. For nurse leaders, caring, compassion, and a commitment to help others help themselves can direct the team to goal attainment (Baginski, 1991). Creating effective teams requires an array of interventions, including the following:

- *Communication.* The leader communicates and translates intentions into reality and sustains the vision.
- *Trust.* The leader places trust in others and understands that trust is the glue that maintains team integrity.
- *Motivation.* The leader strives to create an environment in which team members are empowered, because the leader believes that empowerment is self-induced.

Teamwork does not follow a straight line. Rather, it is a path that takes time, energy, and education. You can achieve balance in your abilities as a team leader by conducting a personal inventory.

Jeffries (1992) suggests that effective leaders have achieved balance in their own lives. This balance comes with the ability to assess oneself as a whole person and identify areas where improvement is required. If you can honestly accept those parts of your life that are unbalanced and improve your personal effectiveness, your leadership capacity is strengthened, and team members benefit. Do not expose or impart the ill effects of personal disharmony onto your team.

> **TIP**
> A stressed and fatigued nurse leader can impede a team's performance.

Complete the Personal Effectiveness Profile (Figure 5.1) to assess your ability to balance life's demands: work, personal, and family obligations.

> **FIGURE 5.1** Personal Effectiveness Profile (Source: Elizabeth Jeffries, 1992. *The Heart of Leadership.* Kendall/Hunt Publishing Co., Dubuque, Iowa.)

Rate yourself from 10 to 100. If you score consistently in the "Needs Improvement" area, ask yourself what steps are necessary to move your score to "Strong" and do something about it!

	Need Improvement 10 20 30	Getting Better 40 50	Good 60 70 80	Strong 90 100
Self-awareness				
Enthusiasm				
Energy				
Positive attitude				
Personal poise				
Active listening				
Self-confidence				
Self-motivation				
Creativeness				
Self-discipline				
Flexibility				
Establishment of goals				
Decision-making skills				
Positive action				
Organizational skills				
Management of time				
Calculated risk taking				
Persistence				
Ambition				
Interest in job				
Public speaking ability				
Vocabulary				
Understanding people				
Management of stress				
Personal relationships				
Concern for others				
Balance of life— Personal, family, career				

As your vision gives hope and your mission direction, you must seek to inspire so others will follow.

THE KEYS TO TEAM BUILDING

1. Build a team that embraces collegial collaboration and uses brainstorming to sort differences. When issues of competition, inequality, and individualism surface, seek support for yourself and team members to avoid division.
2. Listen well and ask open-ended questions, such as "What do you think of the vision?" Call on individual team members to secure their support. Give team members special roles within the team, such as information gatherer or topic specialist. Ensure that the information being communicated within the team is not in dispute and that team members are working from the same data and facts.
3. Keep the team focused. If a team member brings up an unrelated idea, goal, or objective, tell that person you are putting the idea in a "parking lot" for the moment. Arrange another time when the idea can be discussed. If you are attempting to secure commitment from your team to improve performance, productivity, and service to your patients and their families, be patient and persevere. It will take a while for the team to work with you.

DEFINITION OF A TEAM

A team is a group of people who perform work that otherwise could not be accomplished easily, effectively, or efficiently by an individual alone. Katzenback and Smith (1993) define a team as a small group of people with complementary skills who are committed to a purpose, goal, and approach for which they hold themselves accountable.

TIP

Teams usually consist of two to twenty-five members who represent a mixture of individuals with technical, problem-solving, decision-making, and interpersonal skills.

As a team develops and focuses on its designated work, its nurse leader gains a sense of the team's dynamics. This often involves understanding how individuals will blend and succeed within the team. It is sometimes as simple as finding the right people for the right job at the right time. You will create and adjust the workings of the team as you move toward diverse interests and goal achievement. It is, however, necessary for the leader to ensure the team understands the rules for working together and sets a receptive climate for the work to take place.

TEAM BUILDING

Team building is an ongoing process that involves deliberate attention and planned effort.

> **TIP**
> The main action of the team leader is to assist the team in pursuing its objectives and resolving its problems.

The success or failure of a team is often reflected in the degree of energy generated by the nurse leader to provide the coordination, collaboration, and consensus necessary to achieve the organizational goals. For collaboration to occur, team members must feel safe to suggest ideas and generate solutions for problem solving and decision making without fear of reprisal or isolation. Not all ideas or solutions will be the right ones, but the team must be given the support to test the waters. They can agree to disagree, but consensus is the key. It is the agreeing and committing to a plan as a team collectively that counts.

The team building process is built on the notion of team readiness. Is the team ready to engage in strategies for influencing its effectiveness? Figure 5.2 is a checklist for determining readiness.

Team building is not a quick or simple solution to workplace issues or problems. However, team building does provide many benefits for those who are willing to work together.

FIGURE 5.2 Team Readiness Checklist

- ❏ Is the team willing to succeed or fail as a team?
- ❏ Is the team willing to use peer critique as a means of quality control?
- ❏ Is there a climate of trust within the team?
- ❏ Is there room for discussion and clarification over administrative and clinical expectations?
- ❏ Are personal and/or professional awards and rewards defined as components of teamwork?
- ❏ Are team members committed to excellence?
- ❏ Can the team develop its own mission or strategic plan or define short- and long-term goals?
- ❏ Can the team carry out its responsibilities without direct supervision by its leader?
- ❏ Do team members have the necessary administrative, clinical, and interpersonal skills to accomplish the team's mission and job specifications?

THE BENEFITS OF TEAMWORK

- **Reduced costs by increasing productivity without sacrificing quality.**
- **Improved working relationships between leader and followers.**
- **Improved work attitudes and morale.**
- **Improved attendance.**

For team building to succeed, its leader must possess a working knowledge of group dynamics and behavior and understand her role as leader. Team building becomes a successful process when team members are taught the following key behaviors by their leader:

- Honesty, integrity, and trust
- Tolerance and respect
- Free and open communication

As a leader, you have an obligation to set the right example. Lead by your own actions. Team members will have different approaches and perhaps a different logic in seeking solutions to problems. For team building to thrive, you must be prepared to facilitate the building of relationships so as to allow creativity and innovation to flourish. You will need to focus less on describing the task and more on facilitating the process. The key is to create an atmosphere that fosters trust and cooperation.

> **TIP**
>
> Building a team requires sharing the burden of complex and diverse decisions while maximizing individual talent and potential.

As the leader, you have to learn patience and improve your listening skills. You must understand team members' words as a product of their unique cultural context. At this level, listening necessarily becomes quite intense. Nod, lean slightly forward, use the person's name, and use the person's words and phrases to make a connection.

As differences emerge within the team, you must practice total unconditional acceptance of team members. On any given day, you may not like their behavior, but that does not mean that you do not accept them. Reach out and connect. Get people to open up by asking opened questions (questions for which responses are more than a yes or no). Use silence and a pause between words. Ask for more information: "Tell me more about that." Allow team members to feel good about themselves. Maintain your own high self-esteem and help others to build theirs (Scholtes, 1988). Enhancing teamwork requires an understanding of how teams evolve. There are basically three phases that occur as an individual becomes a team member:

1. Personal phase
    Personal belonging
    Orientation
    Membership
    Control and influence
    Support and loyalty
2. Team phase
    Team belonging
    Orientation to team members
    Formulation of relationships

　　　　Role and responsibility
　　　　Communication
　　　　Trust and intimacy
　3. Organizational phase
　　　　Organizational belonging
　　　　Orientation to organization
　　　　Team training and development

Knowing about these phases should help you to relieve much of the emotional and group pressures new team members experience. By helping team members through the phases of orientation, you build cooperation, communication, and cohesion among all team members.

The survival of the team may depend on the establishment of relationships and networks at every phase. The secret to harmonious relationships is the ability of the leader to understand the phases of team orientation and direct skillful collaborative behaviors.

Once the team is fully oriented to its members and mission, you can assess its ability to work as a cohesive unit. Determine what qualities represent the best and worst of your team. It is important to isolate those qualities that destroy team effectiveness and cohesion. Beware of barriers that might interfere with communication and create conflict:

- Preconceived expectations
- Prejudices
- Cherished beliefs
- Need to control
- Lack of clarity of the goal
- Role misconceptions

As misunderstandings occur, encourage team members to bring the matter to the group for discussion. When team members are encouraged, supported, and shown how to deal with conflict openly, they continue on a harmonious path (Dobbs, 1993). By clearing the air of innuendo and suspicion, team members learn to solve problems efficiently and effectively. Team members must understand their role and that of other members in reducing confusion and hostility. Provide direct feedback on interactions that support and promote positive group behaviors. Ask yourself: What does the team need to grow and develop? (See Figure 5.3.)

> **FIGURE 5.3** Team Performance Worksheet

1. List all those qualities that best reflect the team's peak performance.
2. List all those qualities that reflect the team's worst performance.
3. What can you do today to increase your team's effectiveness?
4. How can you encourage peak performance?
5. What can you do to reward peak performance?
6. What will it take to empower team members?

CREATING A WINNING TEAM

First and foremost, teamwork reduces the costs of turnover, recruitment, orientation, and absenteeism. By creating a good place to work, team members experience creative problem solving, greater productivity, and increased personal satisfaction. Smith, Smith, and Olian (1994) suggest that socially integrated teams that use informal communications as well as formal communications have better performance outcomes.

> **TIP**
>
> A key to creating a winning team is to understand their wants.

Ask team members what they desire from the workplace. If you are unsure and insecure about approaching team members, consider asking them to fill out the Workplace Motivation Factors Inventory (Figure 5.4), which lists some key challenges and preferences known to motivate individuals in the workplace. This inventory is completed by placing a numerical value next to each space, with a 1 representing the most important and a 10 rating representing the least important. (You can add items to this inventory.)

SECURING COMMITMENT

All teams eventually experience conflict, misunderstanding, or crisis. A team leader who remains alert will be prepared to reduce confusion and disagreement when it arises. Securing commitment to teamwork and challenging a team's performance requires a well-planned strategy.

Strategies for Managing Teams

- **Provide continuous feedback.**
- **Give frequent recognition.**
- **Provide lots of rewards.**

Give Feedback

State the problem in a clear manner, and be sure to focus on it, not the team member. Connect the problem to the functioning and quality of the organization and to the team member's self-interest. Encourage the team member to bring the reasons for the problem into the open. All concerns should be aired. Ask the team member to offer suggestions and ways on how to solve the problem. Listen openly and free of judgment. Select steps each of you will take to solve the problem. Develop an action plan, and write it down. Set a future date to review progress and reinforce positive behaviors.

Figure 5.4 Workplace Motivation Factors Inventory

Recognition for competence and accomplishments _____

Respect and dignity _____

Financial security _____

Opportunities for decision making _____

Personal choice and job freedom _____

Good work environment _____

Promotion possibilities _____

Open, fair, and consistent manager _____

Congenial team members _____

Good benefits _____

Other: _____

_____

Give Recognition

State what the team member did that deserves recognition, and express your personal satisfaction with the team member. Be sure to use the person's name, and be sincere. Explain why this performance is important, and encourage continued success.

Give Rewards

Keep it simple and clear. Define role expectations and standards. Design an awards program for all levels of the team. Celebrate life events—graduations, engagements, weddings, births—and certifications. Think of ways to promote morale, team spirit, and collegiality.

SUMMARY

Teamwork is the answer to nurse leaders who are facing personnel shortages, financial constraints, and quality care issues. However, trying too hard to turn individual work into teamwork merely for the sake of forming teams is a recipe for chronic distress. For a team to perform well, the leader must be sure to move the team toward its goals. Become an effective strategist:

- Provide the framework and direction for the team's operations.
- Define performance criteria, and determine special competencies.
- Set priorities and timetables.
- Establish the standards and controls necessary to monitor progress.

Any time team members have to ask the team leader, "What do you want us to do?", then teamwork is not working.

Members of an effective team will seek to enhance their professionalism, performance, and productivity with guidance from the team leader. To support the team in these efforts, the nurse leader must be prepared to:

- Inspire with a vision.
- Motivate with a mission.
- Set clear role expectations.
- Be a role model.
- Support and encourage cooperation and coordination.
- Provide praise.
- Celebrate accomplishments.

Nurse leaders who strive to create a climate for teamwork and provide the context, structure, and resources are much more likely to be successful at communicating and leading—and contributing to the development of a winning team. Team leaders can enhance productivity and reduce costs by helping people work together more effectively and make better decisions. In helping individuals, teams, and the organization find healthy and sustainable team-building skills, the leader dramatically alters the situation for the good of patients, families, and the community.

Challenge your team. Find new and better ways of working through teamwork—effective teamwork. Promoting teamwork is not an easy task. A group of people is a team only when its members work together like a finely tuned machine. The interpersonal dynamics of the team must be honed to a razor's edge. Each team member must possess an understanding of her own strengths and weaknesses and be capable of offering personal and professional feedback that is precise yet tactful. Each team member must seek to control her own desires and need for power for the common good.

Teamwork takes a substantial amount of energy and enthusiasm. The team leader's role is to coach and facilitate gently. Be sure to restate the vision and values of the organization frequently. Be persistent. Wear the vision as if it were a part of your clothing. Let it be a constant reminder of why you made a commitment to serve this organization. The results will be well worth the effort.

REFERENCES

Baginski, Y. (1991). The value team approach: Integrating personal and organizational values. *Caring, 10*(10), 26–28, 30, 32.
Bennis, W., and Nanus, B. (1985). *Leaders: The strategies for taking charge.* Harper & Row: New York.
Block, P. (1988). *The empowered manager.* San Francisco: Jossey-Bass.
Dobbs, J. (1993, February). The empowerment environment. *Training and Development,* 47–55.
Gregory, C. (1995). Creating a vision for a nursing unit. *Nursing Management, 26*(1), 38–41.
Jeffries, E. (1992). *The heart of leadership.* Dubuque, IA: Kendall/Hunt Publishing Co.
Holladay, S., and Coombs, W. (1993). Communicating visions: An exploration of the rate of delivery in the creation of leader charisma. *Management Communication Quarterly, 6*(4), 405–427.
Katzenbach, J., and Smith, D. (1993). The discipline of teams. *Harvard Business Review, 71*(2), 111–120.

Meyer, C. (1994). How the right measures help teams excel. *Harvard Business Review, 72*(3), 95–103.

Peters, T. (1994). *The Tom Peters seminar.* New York: Vintage Books.

Scholtes, P. R. (1988). *The team handbook.* Madison, WI: Joiner Associates.

Smith, K. G., Smith, K. A., and Olian, J. D. (1994). Top management team demography and process: The role of social integration and communication. *Administrative Science Quarterly, 39,* 412–438.

Stengel, C. (1992). *The gospel according to Casey: Casey Stengel's inimitable, instructional, historical baseball book.* New York: St. Martin's Press.

CHAPTER 6

Understanding Change

Change is not an event, it is an enjoyable and rewarding journey.
JAMES A. BELASCO (1990)

In today's world change is dramatic and fast-paced, and the problems may seem complex and overwhelming. Yet opportunities for securing improvement in the health care system have never before been greater. Nurse leaders must be prepared to address basic human needs and develop successful strategies for change. Confronted with rising cost, a growing uninsured population, and an overbedded health care system, nurse leaders must be a driving force behind change within the health care system.

The accelerating pace of change demands constant vigilance. Nurse leaders must be prepared to help followers cope with a downsized, reengineered, and restructured health care system. The challenge is to become proactive and responsive to change and policy development, not accept business as usual. Nurse leaders must strive to facilitate the change process with creative, intellectual leadership.

TIP

Nurse leaders must be poised to diagnose situations, capabilities, and needs, and then plot an appropriate course of action that will deliver the highest payoff through straightforward communication.

THE CHANGE PROCESS

Change will occur whether you want it or not. It is a complex process involving many structures with varying interpersonal responses and needs. The never-ending challenge for nurse leaders is to be an effective guide through the change process. Kanter (1985) defines change as the crystallization of new action possibilities based on reconceptualized patterns in the organization. A **change** is a deviation from an established pattern; it requires creating a new system.

By nature, we are creatures of habit and find comfort in steady relationships, and familiar technologies, and the environment in general. Who wants disruption, upheaval, modification, or change? It is the responsibility of nurse leaders to clarify the need for change. Start with making a case for change:

- Identify new health care trends and scenarios.
- Examine current health care challenges.
- Explore market demands.
- Define performance gaps.
- Contemplate the consequences of not acting or making changes.

Although change is difficult, there is a set of principles applicable to virtually every planned-change program.

Principles of Change

1. The change process must be based on patient-customer values.
2. View the change as a set of processes that cut horizontally across the organization to serve the patient-customer.
3. Think broadly. Consider how technology, people, and processes act together and separately to influence change.
4. Do not be constrained by tradition. Be open and willing to learn from others, both internal and external to the organization.
5. Look at the full contribution and value of all those involved in the change process.
6. Focus resources where the real value is created.
7. Build a foundation for continuous improvement by tracking and communicating progress and results.

In the face of rapid and high-intensity change, knowledge of and skill in the use of the change process is important.

Becoming a Change Agent

Nurse leaders must learn to anticipate impending change, respond to it, and take action to direct its course. They must also understand how people cope with change. Sheehan (1990) suggests that **change agents** serve at least three important functions: (1) a precursor function, by preparing the way for change; (2) a facilitator function by enabling change to happen; and (3) a function in identifying and repairing breakdowns when they occur. As a change agent, help those around you to become more self-directing, self-empowered, and less dependent on external direction.

Tips on Facilitating Change

1. **Realize what followers affected by the change are experiencing.** Do not argue with them over their feelings or be surprised by strong negative reactions. For many, a change causes a loss of identity, and they are reacting to that loss.
2. **Talk through the change.** Help followers sort out what is going on. Be prepared to provide information about the who, what, when, where, why, and how of change. And do not just say it once and expect followers to get it. Follow the 7 × 7 rule: Say it seven times in seven different ways.
3. **Anticipate grief.** Expect grieving, shock, denial, anger, bargaining, anxiety, and sadness. Openly acknowledge the loss of the old way of doing things.
4. **Acknowledge a period of confusion.** Followers will experience a sort of neutral zone after the loss, so do not be surprised when they go through a period of confusion or depression.
5. **Expect resistance.** It is a natural reaction to change.

Laying the Groundwork

How do you gear up and run with change? The following suggestions offer insight on laying the groundwork for a planned change:

1. Insist on support from the top. Senior executives must be prepared and able to say, "This is what has to be done, and this is what it will look like in the end," and then continually emphasize the rationale for the change.
2. Be prepared to differentiate between strategic issues (doing right things) and operational issues (doing things right). Strategic issues must come first; they form the basis for top management's decisions. Strategic issues can be identified by asking such questions as: What do patients really value? How will our health care delivery services

change in the future? Which nursing services should receive our highest attention? Where is our competitive advantage?

3. Be prepared to carve out appropriate responsibilities for everyone involved in the change process. For example, top managers might be responsible for developing a clear vision, establishing strategic goals, and identifying and prioritizing core processes. Middle managers might be responsible for building cross-functional teams, planning for the appropriate training, and setting specific targets, goals, and guidelines for determining realistic standards of care. Team members might be responsible for the application of change concepts and tools to analyze the target change processes and propose alternatives as needed.

4. Schedule and divide the training programs for the change into digestible segments that emphasize learning by doing. For the change to be incorporated into daily operations, you need to move the team toward implementation. Small, frequent training sessions offer team members the ability to participate in the process and understand what must be changed.

5. Encourage team members to define and redesign the change processes as needed so as to improve performance and productivity. Insist on defining the scope of the change by asking: Is sufficient information being provided about the change? What information must be received? What information must be produced? What information must be given to someone else?

6. Insist that team members share ideas. Have team members present ideas, thoughts, and results. By delivering a presentation, team members help to structure the experience and better understand the functions and responsibilities required. Sharing of team members' ideas and results enhances communication and dialogue among all those involved in the change process.

7. Develop a culture of inclusion and ownership. Team members need to become architects and owners of the change because they are the ones who must execute the process.

8. Avoid the immediate jump in a planned change without understanding the solution. To help ensure a rational, cost-effective solution, be sure you are clear on what information people need to know.

TIP

To be an effective change agent, be prepared to know the who, what, when, and how of the change.

PLANTING THE SEED

For any change to occur, there must be a need to change and a belief that change is possible. Nurse leaders must first create the urgency to change. Ask yourself how you can create the urgency or desire to change. You might examine the clinical environment—the people, politics, policies, processes, and patients—and identify symptoms that reflect inadequate performance or productivity:

- Increase in patient complaints
- Increase in patient falls
- Increase in medication errors
- Increase in nosocomial infections
- Low staff morale
- Increase in budget variances
- Decrease in patient teaching and documentation

HOW TO DEMONSTRATE CHANGE IS NEEDED

- **Share the unfavorable results of patient surveys, letters, and complaints with team members.**
- **Display unit or service performance and productivity numbers on the bulletin board (good and bad).**
- **Display articles, newspaper clippings, and pictures that draw attention to issues of morale, motivation, and teamwork.**
- **Hold frequent staff meetings to open the lines of communication.**

Both symbols and words will transform the need to change into a clear message of action and improvement:

- Demonstrate through budget analysis or variances what it costs to operate the unit or service.
- Show each team member what it costs to do that person's job.
- Create control measures and monitor performance.

Finally, to pave the way for change to occur:

- Develop a clear picture of what you want.
- Show your team how to do better.
- Be a role model, and help team members to adopt new behaviors.

- Visit and speak with team members and patients frequently.
- Handle complaints quickly.
- Seek input about the impending changes.
- Listen actively to the inputs.
- Reinforce and reward new, improved behaviors.

Creating a Change Strategy

To help your team better understand the concept of change and how to implement it, you must create a strategy. That strategy has to connect the purpose of the change to a commitment to patient satisfaction and service, along with a team commitment to excellence as the driving force.

No successful strategic change occurs in isolation; rather, it is a collective achievement that requires much energy and commitment from multiple stakeholders. Hutt, Walker, and Frankwick (1995) suggest that successful change comes about after confronting the three common barriers to it: turf, interpretative (what is the meaning of the *change* to an individual), and communication. Once a nurse leader recognizes these barriers, she can assess the effect of change on stakeholders and identify zones of support and opposition.

By acknowledging the barriers of change and the skills needed to overcome them, you reduce the forces inhibiting the change. Use the barriers as a way to plan and create an environment that seeks to match the individual with the opportunity to change. For example, if the planned change means that two services or departments will now share personnel or financial resources, open up lines of communication through e-mail correspondence, face-to-face meetings or other formal mechanisms. Ineffective communication and turf battles should not prevent you from implementing a change.

Tips for Creating a Winning Strategy

1. **Establish a sense of urgency. Make a case for action or even create a crisis to galvanize support.**
2. **Create a vision. Establish a positive vision for the future, and focus on a few processes that are critical to the change.**
3. **Empower others to act on the vision. Actively involve everyone in the change process.**
4. **Plan for success. Set clear and measurable goals. Know how to consolidate improvements, and continuously monitor change efforts.**

As a nurse leader, you must amass a reservoir of relevant information. The assembling and analysis data allows the system to provide and deliver services in response to patient-customer needs.

> **TIP**
>
> Your role as change agent is to create an organizational climate or culture that values improvement driven by patient need.

To ensure preparedness for seizing opportunities to change, Kanter (1989) identifies three tools necessary to support change and innovation: information, support, and resources.

Using Communication

Given the major demands and impact that change has on team members, there must be a plan for communicating the change. The **communication plan** is a map that sets out the objectives, implications, training requirements, and progress reports of the planned change (Bolton, Adydin, Poplow, and Rammsayer, 1992). It details the key message, message timing, and frequency of needed communications.

To devise a plan, first assess and analyze how your team has received messages on changes in the past. Be sensitive to how messages are translated and perceived.

The Communication Plan

- *Invest adequate resources into the communication effort.* Use the telephone, bulletin board, e-mail, and monthly newsletters to alert and inform all those involved in the change process.
- *Invest in a one-page colored memo format.* Frequent messages in a simple format are best. Keep the message clear and concise. Use bright paper to get attention.
- *Invest in one-to-one targeted meetings.* Use personal oral communication to augment written forms by targeting key individuals vital to the change process. Schedule these meetings every two to three weeks to support and encourage the change efforts.

- *Personalize communications as much as possible.* **Be prepared to spend a significant amount of time allaying fears and anxieties. Change never becomes meaningful until individuals are made to realize lives will change.** By communicating in special and personal ways, you can reduce misunderstandings and promote trust during the change process.
- *Communicate the right message in the right way.* **Be ready to deliver the message in any way your team will best receive it. Stop and ask yourself what format each communication should take: written memo or personal presentation?**

By using a well-developed communication plan, you can quickly gauge the success or shortcomings of your targeted change. When you seek out ways to communicate openly with those directly involved in the change process, you better understand how to modify and improve the change.

The Human Aspect

Change efforts fail if the needs of people are not met. Nurse leaders must help identify what people need to be more adaptable and flexible toward change. Silber (1993) suggests that tampering with the status quo threatens the security of basic needs and may turn it into fear.

> **TIP**
>
> Helping people successfully weather the change process is the cornerstone to lasting achievement.

The first step is to understand the various needs experienced by people in the organization. If these needs are not met, productivity will be affected and resistance triggered. An assessment of individual needs can help nurse leaders develop an action plan for effectively involving people in the change process. Consider the needs that most people are concerned with during the change process:

- Security
- Power
- Rules and regulations
- Relationships

When implementing change, never leave the human aspect to chance. Act thoughtfully, use good judgment and critical thinking, and be sure all decisions are well developed. Avoid haste in doing and deciding as it relates to the change. Act enthusiastically. Positive energy produces action. Enthusiasm will be more attractive to team members than rules and power. Positive results will unfold when individuals themselves discover the benefits of change rather than being told what the change must or will produce. Relationships will flourish when calmness and serenity are encouraged over conventional strategies of timetables, cost factors, and political favors.

Keeping the human aspect of change on the table during implementation helps nurse leaders to secure cooperation and foster confidence in those participating in the change. Cooperation and confidence lead to accomplishment. It is the nurse leader's responsibility to facilitate high performance and break through resistance as the change is implemented.

A number of factors may lead to resistance:

- Threatened self-interest
- Inaccurate perceptions
- Objective disagreement
- Low tolerance for change
- A psychological reaction toward anything new or different

Once these factors are identified, nurse leaders can develop a framework for overcoming resistance and map strategies that will lead to an ongoing process of discovery, reflection, and renewal. Approach resistance by keeping the focus on what is most important: your bottom line (the issue), not your ego. Understand your instinctive approach to conflict and criticism. Be careful not to take the resistance personally.

Analyze your power base in the change process. Seek to maintain high standards for quality and performance through rewards and recognition, not threats and punishment. Know your hot buttons, and realize resistance will emerge regardless of how prepared you are to deal with it.

To guide your team through the change process in a way that enhances learning and leads to successful implementation, you must allow the change to be:

- Focused
- Flexible
- Friendly
- Fun

Help your team achieve success with change by providing the necessary education and support. Use an outside consultant or agent with expertise to assist in the educational process when needed.

> **TIP**
>
> Consider introducing the change as a pilot project or providing for a gradual introduction to less resistance, and allow for greater learning and discovery. Remember that implementing change—any change—is really about learning.

As a nurse leader, you must begin to value and appreciate the different ways of behaving and operating when change is planned and implemented. The key is to become a trusted partner in helping others to sustain success during change. Begin by increasing their ability to learn, change, and achieve their highest capability through:

- Promoting integrity and honesty.
- Valuing diversity.
- Combining analytical and intuitive processes.
- Creating a caring environment.
- Providing incentives and rewards for successful changes.

Do not expect to see quick results and motivated team members. Your strategy must be to help your team recognize and understand the concept of change and how to deliver it.

A Shift in Mind-Set

The shift to change as a way of achieving excellence or continuing improvement in clinical care is nothing less than a complete shift in mind-set. Nurse leaders must begin to see that the change process is part of their business of leadership and directing patient-focused care.

Key Elements for Mapping Change

- *Environmental:* The physical setting of the change.
- *Aesthetic:* The sensory experience that the change will have. It can include sights, sounds, odors, and physical sensations.

- *Interpersonal:* The interaction of staff, patients, and families. This component includes friendliness, helpfulness, and physical appearance, and competence.
- *Procedural:* The procedures necessary to accomplish the change. They may include filling out forms, providing information, explaining needs, going to meetings or various locations, and using new equipment.
- *Informational:* How the team members get the information they need to function. This component may include oral or written instructions concerning the change.
- *Deliverable:* Any item given to the team for use in the change process, such as special equipment, tools, or documents.
- *Financial:* How much and in what way the change saves (or costs) the organization money.

CHANGE AND PROBLEM SOLVING

Once a commitment to change is made, nurse leaders must use a systematic approach to plan change and solve problems. To help teams and individuals avoid some of the common pitfalls of ineffective change and problem solving, consider the following traps:

- Jumping too quickly toward a conclusion before exploring all the aspects of the problem.
- Failing to obtain critical facts, about either the problem or proposed change.
- Selecting problems or changes that are too general, too complex, or poorly defined.
- Failing to articulate a rational solution to the problem or proposed change.
- Failing to implement and evaluate the proposed change appropriately.

The **problem-solving process** is a strategy for nurse leaders to use in resolving problems and promoting change. (Appendix A contains the steps for designing a planned change.) A general process for making change in systems, work process, management process, and organizational conditions, it fosters:

- Clear definition of the problem
- Analysis of data
- Understanding of causes

- Creation of ideas
- Teamwork
- Commitment

Duck (1993) suggests that the key tasks in change are managing the dynamic, connecting, and balancing all the pieces.

THE PROBLEM-SOLVING PROCESS

1. *Identify and select the problem.* **What do we want to change?**
2. *Analyze the problem.* **What is preventing us from reaching the desired state?**
3. *Generate potential solutions.* **How could we make the change?**
4. *Select and plan the solution.* **What is the best way to do it?**
5. *Implement the solution.* **Are we following the plan?**
6. *Evaluate the solution.* **How well did it work?**

Another helpful approach to planning change is to map the process from beginning to end (see Figure 6.1 on pages 88–89).

CELEBRATING CHANGE

There are preconditions for managing change successfully: realistic expectations, commitment by senior management, a shared vision, and employee involvement. To succeed in change efforts, nurse leaders must be in a position to command respect and resources. They have to have the stamina to pull it off, as well as the perseverance to overcome resistance. Once the fundamentals of getting people to pull together are fully recognized and conditions are created to accomplish the change, nurse leaders must provide time to celebrate. This means rewarding those who were committed to taking risks, being innovative, and designing new solutions.

SUMMARY

Change is constant and inevitable, and its pace is accelerating. Thus, the real issue for nurse leaders is whether the change will happen belatedly, in a crisis atmosphere, or with foresight, in a cool, calm, and considered manner.

The objective in change is a transformation that is revolutionary in result and evolutionary in execution.

Facilitating the change process is a key responsibility of nurse leaders. To get ahead of the change curve, you must look around the organization. Pay attention to the services, products, and policies that have recently been launched. Identify the issues confronting you or preoccupying your time. Examine your record of innovation and new business concepts. Look into the faces of team members, peers, and patients. Stop and contemplate their fears. Now look toward the future, and ponder your ability to change and shape that future in the years to come.

Ask yourself:

- Are you ready to assume the responsibilities of a good change agent?
- Do you have a clear understanding of how health care may be different ten years from now?
- Are you aware of which health care issues or problems absorb most of your attention?
- Do you possess the necessary leadership and change style for organization restructuring and redesign?
- Are you positioned for these changes?

These are not merely rhetorical questions. The capacity to anticipate changing environmental and client needs, to act, and to allay concerns for the future is not the province solely of nurse leaders; members from all levels of the health care team can help create change. Nurse leaders, however, must take responsibility for establishing a solid foundation before introducing any change effort. To initiate change successfully, nurse leaders must stay flexible by evaluating barriers to change, keeping an open mind to new methods, technologies, and techniques, and periodically assessing progress in facilitating successful change.

The key in initiating successful change is flexibility. Nurse leaders with the capacity and ability to bend without breaking can adapt to or respond to change as well as be influenced by the process itself. Creating and building a perspective that is flexible includes developing a consensus about the purpose, scope, and process of change.

Understanding change and viewing the process with less ambiguity can help nurse leaders strengthen the organization's vision. It can also serve to motivate and empower team members to grow with the changes, meet with the forces of resistance, and create new ways of dealing positively with change (Perlman and Takacs, 1990).

FIGURE 6.1 Mapping the Problem-Solving Process

I. Describe the current state of the problem.
   1. Define the issues clearly and concisely.
   2. List the contributing forces and causes.
   3. Define what is working well and opportunities.
   4. Define what is not working.

II. Describe the desired state.
   1. Fully address all the issues surrounding the problem: people, process, and procedure.
   2. Define the required changes.
   3. Clarify optimal roles for each team member.
   4. Seek to open and improve communication.
   5. Beware of the heightened anxiety among team members, and reduce stress.
   6. Develop new and different way to cooperate and collaborate.
   7. Revisit the organization's mission and standards of practice.
   8. Encourage a commitment toward increased service quality.

III. Define what needs to change.
   1. Identify the gaps between the current state and the desired state.
   2. Assign primary responsibilities to key team members.

IV. Develop a change strategy and a plan on how to implement the change.
   1. Design a work plan.
   2. Develop an effective communication network to announce the change.
   3. Encourage and seek the involvement of all team members.
   4. Provide ongoing support throughout the change process with special tokens of appreciation.
   5. Deal with resistance openly and honestly.

V. Implement and change.
   1. Provide assistance and support during the transition phase of the change process.
   2. Define outcomes of the change, and measure progress along the way.
   3. Provide continuous reinforcement and support.
   4. Be prepared to make a course correction as the change proceeds.

VI. Hold ongoing planning meetings with the team.
   1. Conduct review sessions to revise change documents and to define successes.

CHAPTER 6 UNDERSTANDING CHANGE **89**

FIGURE 6.1 *continued*

   2. Redefine roles, expectations, and accountabilities as necessary.
   3. Clarify communications, outline, and content of changes as the need dictates.
   4. Determine relevant data, information available, and useful documents to support the change.
   5. Identify key players whose support is required.
VII. Collect and analyze data.
   1. Schedule and conduct interviews and focus groups.
   2. Distribute questionnaires (if appropriate).
   3. Conduct research and benchmarking.
   4. Complete initial analysis and develop preliminary findings.
   5. Review progress and initial findings.
   6. Determine course corrections and changes.
   7. Determine key communications required and updates.
VIII. Complete the analysis, and develop conclusions and recommendations.
   1. Determine the most effective interventions and changes.
   2. Create the preliminary communications and implementation plan.
   3. Review and revise recommendations.
   4. Determine whether additional analysis is required.
   5. Test alternatives.
   6. Develop communications and next steps.
IX. Develop an implementation plan.
   1. Develop a timetable.
   2. Identify key players and accountabilities.
   3. Identify problems, implications, barriers, and solutions.
   4. Establish milestones, and assign primary responsibilities for tasks and changes.
   5. Create an overall strategy for change.
X. Prepare follow-up and progress reviews.
   1. Teach new skills and attitudes.
   2. Measure and evaluate change indicators.
   3. Reinforce and support new behaviors and attitudes.
   4. Make a course correction if indicated.

The challenge for nurse leaders in these unsettled times is to remain positive, flexible, enthusiastic, and energetic. The more nurse leaders exercise their freedom to choose a response toward change, the more proactive they will become. Being proactive toward change feeds opportunities and starves problems, avoids excuses, and focuses attention on doing the right things.

References

Belasco, J. (1990). *Teaching the elephant to dance: Empowering change in your organization.* New York: Crown Publisher.
Duck, J. D. (1993). Managing change: The art of balance. *Harvard Business Review, 71,* 109–118.
Hutt, M., Walker, B., and Frankwick, B. (1995). Hurdle the cross-functional barriers to strategic change. *Sloan Management Review, 36*(3), 22–30.
Kanter, R. M. (1989). *When giants learn to dance: mastering the challenge of strategy, management, and careers in the 1990's.* New York: Simon and Schuster.
Kanter, R. M. (1985). *The change masters: innovation for productivity in the american corporation.* New York: Simon and Schuster.
Sheehan, J. (1990). Investigating change in a nursing context. *Journal of Advanced Nursing, 15,* 819–824.
Silber, M. (1993). The "C" in excellence: Choices and change. *Nursing Management, 24*(9), 60–62.

CHAPTER 7
Facilitating the Group Process

A wise leader knows each of his followers; he knows when and how to deliver information to each of them.

ELIZABETH JEFFRIES (1992)

Leading groups and managing their behavior is a deliberate and strategic act. The appropriate use of group process skills by nurse leaders will contribute to the effectiveness of communication, member relationships, and productivity within groups. Facilitation is the most important skill for nurse leaders to develop. It requires thoughtful but simple planning.

QUALITIES OF PRIMARY FACILITATORS

- **Sensitive to the emotions of the group.**
- **Able to gauge the energy levels and stress tolerance of the group.**
- **Able to be a role model while nuturing groups through shared responsibilities.**

Learning the nuts and bolts of how groups work can yield tremendous dividends in group effectiveness and productivity. The process of achieving group effectiveness begins with an evaluation of the group.

MEASURING GROUP EFFECTIVENESS

- **Can each member speak and really be listened to often enough to feel a sense of belonging and ownership?**
- **Does having this group in your life make you feel empowered and challenge you?**

- Do you look forward to group meetings with your team, or is it just a chore?
- Can you be honest with this group? For example, can you express your anger? frustration?
- Does belonging to this group give you a positive identity?
- Does the group open easily to new members and acknowledge the departure of old members?
- Do you feel accepted by the group as their facilitator?
- Does this group bring out the best in you?
- Do group members challenge and make you stretch beyond what you thought you were capable of?
- Do you experience a balance between what you are contributing and what you are receiving from the group?

By answering these questions, the nurse leader begins to uncover the many benefits of belonging to a group. **Facilitators** have the capacity to help group members grow and develop a psychic bond that promotes unity and a special connectedness that goes beyond the nature of the work.

THE NATURE OF GROUP WORK

Nurse leaders must take into consideration the nature of group work when planning any interaction. Although any particular group interaction may differ from others, each group is different and must be considered for its strengths and weaknesses.

GROUP VARIABLES

- *Group members.* Give serious consideration to the similarities and differences in knowledge, skill, ability, and attributes among group members.
- *Purpose and goals.* Identify the reasons for the group's coming together. The overall purpose and goals need to be clearly stated since they will have an impact on the group's planning.
- *Workplace atmosphere and environment.* Create a positive and productive atmosphere, a concept that encompasses the physical surroundings, the room temperature, patterns of communication, and interpersonal interactions. The right atmosphere, designed with careful thought and consideration, can foster greater participation and productivity.

- *Work priorities.* Clearly explain work priorities, responsibilities, and duties to be achieved by group members. Consider work assignments, schedules, and processes to achieve favorable patient outcomes.
- *Staying connected.* All group work requires continuous communication and follow-up. Stay closely aligned to the group and its work. This means knowing the successes and failures of group work. By sending thank-you notes and e-mail or making telephone calls, you send a message that you care. Continuous coaching can have many forms, but the purpose is essentially the same: to reach out and let group members know you are aware of the issues, problems, and outcomes of their work.

BECOMING A FACILITATOR

A group facilitator is a nurse leader who helps a group free itself from the obstacles or barriers to everyday work.

THE FACILITATOR'S ROLE

- Guiding without directing.
- Making changes without disruption.
- Helping others to self-discover new approaches and solutions to problems.
- Breaking down barriers between individuals.
- Learning to appreciate diversity and differences among group members.

THE ART OF FACILITATION

To facilitate effectively, nurse leaders must listen to and observe the ebb and flow of group activity and work. Becoming familiar with the interactive skills of the group provides the insight needed to select the best course of action given the group's energy level. Facilitation is a sequential process:

1. Initiate contact.
    - Be sensitive to the group's feelings, thoughts, and emotions.
    - Be aware of how the group collects facts and interprets its findings.
    - Know how the group problem solves and finds solutions.

2. Build and nurture interpersonal skills.
   - The first contact is the most important contact.
   - Be open and free to listen. Avoid giving advice.
   - Give assistance by building on others' ideas or proposals to arrive at consensus.
   - Seek to increase mutual understanding and foster a dialogue on the issues of concern.
   - Be ready with supportive reactions that demonstrate agreement with the group's thoughts, ideas, and feelings.
   - Be realistic and offer disagreeing reactions when the group's proposals or issues are not responsive or responsible to the organization's vision and values.
   - Be careful when the group's emotions lead to defending or attacking reactions. These reactions are value judgments and often made with an angry or hostile overtone by an individual group member.
3. Move beyond behavior to action. As the group sets priorities in work activities, encourage freedom of thought among group members. In the spirit of practicing the art of facilitation, offer facts, data, or clarification when asked.
   - Avoid assuming responsibility for developing solutions and making decisions for the group. This will reduce the chances of an emotional explosion or confrontation. Seek only to share essential information relevant to the issue or activity at hand to provide a perspective on the fiscal constraints as well as the authority necessary to act.
   - Share expectations of what will be accomplished and by what standards.
   - Clarify misunderstandings and stress the constructive aspects of the situation.
   - Incorporate mutual interests so as to increase the motivation of all group members.

Facilitating Feelings

All nurse leaders will eventually be confronted with the personal feelings of an individual group member as it relates to a particular situation or issue. Through careful planning and foresight, you can handle unexpected strong feelings:

- Stay calm. Try not to become frightened or panic.
- Be attentive to negative feelings and address them.
- Be prepared to deal with the emotions at the moment by providing acceptable outlets.

There will be many occasions when group members will not see eye to eye with each other or their nurse leader. The leader can facilitate and help group members express their feelings:

- *Accept the expression of feelings rather than disagreeing with or rejecting them.* Acceptance conveys an attitude that the ideas or thoughts presented are worthy of attention. Facilitators do not have to agree with the idea, only listen openly. Be patient and thank the group member for his or her thoughts. Remain nonjudgmental and identify what was significant and meaningful to the discussion.
- *Be sensitive to expressions of anger and resentment.* Be aware of verbal and nonverbal cues of group members. There cues are often loaded with emotion and if not addressed will prevent the group from moving forward. You must be ready to handle the feelings of the group first before attending to the tasks at hand. If feelings are ignored, members may withdraw from the discussion and become passive observers.
- *Focus on understanding feelings first.* Try to suspend judgment on why the group feels a certain way. Be open and try to understand the facts surrounding the situation. Seek additional information; ask the group members if they understand the content and feelings of what is occurring at the moment. Clarify the messages by reflecting on the words being used, and address the true feelings of the group. Summarize where the group stands on the particular issue, sort out the confusion, and allow the misunderstandings to emerge.

The Facilitator's Role

Assuming the role of a primary facilitator of a group or a team requires key behaviors on the part of nurse leaders.

BEHAVIORS ESSENTIAL TO GROUP PROCESS

- **Build the group into a cohesive whole that allows for improved decision making.**
- **Support group development by using efficient communication processes to improve the exchange of information, facts, and knowledge for patient care delivery.**
- **Encourage group decision making at every opportunity, and promote the concept of self-managed groups.**

- **Provide a supportive climate** for maintaining the health and well-being of the group through teaching group members to share in this responsibility.
- **Foster autonomy and creativity** of ideas and solutions by helping group members gain confidence and security in sharing ideas, thoughts, and opinions with each other.

Promoting Group Openness and Participation

For group members to feel confident and safe to contribute effectively, nurse leaders must create a participative climate. To ensure that members feel secure and desire to participate fully, try using open-ended questions to initiate the process.

> **TIP**
> Ask questions that begin with *how, what,* and *why.*

The following types of questions will help group members easily seek or give information rather than answering with a yes or no:

Direct Question.   Leads to a response from a specific group member. *Example:* "Ms. Clark, what do you think about the new information system?"

General Question.   Leads to a response from any group member. *Example:* "How should we arrange the vacation schedule to cover summer requests?"

Return Question.   Leads to returning to the group member who asked the question. This technique allows the person asking the question to elaborate more fully than the question indicates. *Example:* "Mary, you asked how to tackle the vacation schedule. Where would you like to begin?"

Relay Question.   Leads to the inclusion of those in the group who have not contributed or those who know the facts a chance to respond to the question. *Example:* "Laura, you have been working with holiday and vacation schedules for a while. Please tell the group what has been successful in the past."

Seeking Consensus and Managing Differences

Reaching consensus is often easier said than done. Before full agreement can be achieved on any level, the voices of different group members must be heard, given full attention, and evaluated. Disagreement and diversity are a natural outcome of group process. Conger (1993) suggests "that future leaders will need to be sensitive to issues of diversity, interpersonally competent, and community builders" (p. 49).

> **TIP**
>
> Nurse leaders are responsible for managing and resolving constructively the differences among group members.

STRATEGIES FOR ENSURING HARMONY

1. **Understand all group members' positions and work to resolve areas of diversity of opinion.**
   - Summarize the different perspectives offered by group members.
   - Use a chalkboard or flip chart to document all responses. Be sure each one is accurately written and reflects the viewpoint as stated by the group member.
   - Review each idea and look for common themes.
2. **Identify and agree on common themes and ideas.** List all of the areas where group agreement has been achieved. Common agreement may be met in the following areas:
   - *Goals:* Does the group agree on what outcome is needed?
   - *Roles:* Does the group agree on who can or should do what?
   - *Methods:* Does the group agree on the method for achieving the goals, solving the problem, or making decisions?
   - *Timing:* Does the group agree on when actions should be decided or completed?
3. **Reduce and define differences.**
   - Sort out all of the areas where disagreement exists.
   - Seek to clarify the major points of conflict.
   - Use a chalkboard or flip chart to isolate and identify the differing viewpoints. This process helps to evaluate the differences more objectively and reduces the strong emotions of ownership by group members.

Once the nurse leader has clearly guided the group through the process of acknowledging differences, the group can move on to explore and define those sources: differing information? conflicting values? varied past experiences? misunderstandings? After the sources have been defined, the nurse leader can move the group to resolve the differences considered the most important.

> **TIP**
>
> Nurse leaders must foster the understanding that diversity of opinion is a positive outcome of group process.

FACILITATING DIVERSITY

- **Address different ideas and perspectives so the group gains a better understanding of the issues and their implications.**
- **Allow different ideas to emerge so the group has many more potential alternatives to choose from.**
- **Attend to every group member's ideas and thoughts.**
- **Generate energy and effort toward the resolution of the issue, problem, or task.**

The key to addressing diversity effectively within the group is to create a constructive means for channeling it. When a conflict or disruptive situation emerges, the nurse leader guides the discussion toward the best solution for the group. Attempts must be made to dissuade personal attacks or allow a group member to get his or her own way. Disruptive behavior breeds negative energy and bad feelings within the group. By contrast, fostering a constructive understanding that disagreements often stem from involvement with the issue and from a personal perspective will encourage the group to be supportive of others' ideas. This awareness will improve the quality of the decisions made by the group and promote a sense of team spirit and a greater commitment to group goals.

> **TIP**
>
> Nurse leaders work as contructivists to facilitate conversation among group members, thus enabling new meanings and solutions to problems to evolve (Davis and Cox, 1994).

Group Meetings

A key activity for nurse leaders is conducting group meetings.

Preparation

Before a leader can think about the process aspects of the meeting, attention and effort should focus on five questions:

1. Is a meeting necessary, or is there another way to obtain the information or tackle the issue? Think about alternatives other than face-to-face meetings:
   - E-mail
   - Telephone calls
   - Memos
   - Informal conversations
2. What are the purposes and desired outcomes of the meeting? The purpose of a meeting is the reason it is being scheduled. Be ready to state clearly why this meeting is going to be held. The following situations usually require a group meeting:
   - No one individual has all the necessary information to make a decision.
   - Acceptance of the decision by group members is necessary to its implementation.
   - The problem or issue is unstructured. Decisions must be made on what information is required, where to find it, how to find it, and so forth.
   - Information needs to be communicated and feedback obtained on the problem or issue.
3. Who should attend the meeting? When preparing the attendance list, consider only those essential to achieving the purpose of meeting. To determine who should be present, ask the following questions:
   - Does the person possess the necessary information, knowledge, or expertise?
   - Will the person be affected by and/or asked to implement the decision or outcomes of the meeting?
   - Will the person assist in the final decision?
   - Does the person need to acquire the knowledge or skill being shared?
   - Will the person act as a credible representative for the group, thus keeping the size down without compromising the group productivity?

4. What is the chemistry of the group members? This issue is very important since it will affect how the meeting is facilitated. Prior to the meeting, consider the following questions:
   - What group members possess the greatest power and influence based on their knowledge, expertise, status, and tenure?
   - What are the group members' similarities and differences as they relate to education, experience, and interest?
   - Which group members will display interest and enthusiasm about attending the meeting? Who will be least interested in attending?
   - What will be the general demeanor of the group (open, responsive, aggressive, passive, intellectual, analytical)?
5. What are the specific agenda topics of the meeting: the purpose, desired outcomes, topics, and time frame? Sometimes the agenda will be built at the start of the meeting. Be flexible and be prepared for whatever the situation calls for. Prioritize each of the agenda items, and determine how each will be addressed. Set a time frame and estimate how much time is required for each item. Is the item just for information purposes, or does it require work or a decision? Prior to the meeting, an agenda should be sent to each group member and should include the following items:
   - Name of the person calling the meeting
   - List of group members invited to the meeting
   - Date, starting and ending times
   - Place of meeting
   - Purpose of meeting

Once the preliminary items are complete—agenda, room setup, flip chart, supplies, notification of participants—the nurse leader can assign roles to group members to enable each one to become an active participant. Here is a list of suggested roles that can be used when a group meeting is called for:

Leader. Responsible for the agenda, directing the group, and managing the meeting. The nurse leader guides the group members to attain the objectives for the meeting.

Timekeeper. Helps keep the group on schedule by monitoring how long the group is taking to accomplish each agenda item and giving regular updates to group members about the progress they are making with the agenda.

Secretary. Performs recorder duties (does the minutes), summarizes, and clarifies.

Facilitator. Acts as a catalyst and helps the group by breaking down barriers or obstacles to group process.

Meeting Dynamics

As facilitator, the nurse leader must attend to three issues:

1. *Uniting the group.* This means promoting harmony within the group by keeping group members' energy and emotions on an even keel. It includes recognizing feelings and working them through, allowing aggression and anger to be expressed, keeping to the purpose of the meeting and sticking to the facts, not taking sides, and handling conflict.
2. *Focusing the group.* As the meeting progresses, the nurse leader must stay alert, bring wanderers back to the point, test for understanding, bring others in who are not participating, summarize, paraphrase, and affirm that the group is on track.
3. *Mobilizing the group.* As the group progresses through the agenda items, the nurse leader must encourage everyone to speak up; this includes protecting the weaker members and keeping the stronger ones under control. When items and issues come on the table for a vote, the nurse leader must get the group to work toward a decision and come to consensus. Once a consensus is reached, the outcome should be recorded. Take care of any leftover issues. Review the outcome of the meeting.

After the meeting, the nurse leader must be sure to identify who is to do what, clearly spelling out responsibilities and duties. If there is a need for a follow-up meeting, then highlight agenda items for the next meeting.

Resolving Conflict

In and of itself, conflict is not destructive. Confrontation often brings difficult issues and problems to the table and forces the group members to come to terms with them. In this sense, conflict is healthy; it fosters creativity, relieves stress, and stimulates resolution. But when the conflict fails to maximize the benefits and talents of group members, it becomes dysfunctional.

Dysfunctional conflict is disruptive and counterproductive, and it destroys group process. It will often emerge from group members who experience differences in values, perspectives, and feelings toward problem solving or other workplace issues. And when resources are scarce, competition within the group will emerge as a major source of conflict.

The group facilitator will have to confront the dysfunctional conflict and manage it from the start. This can be a tricky task because you must simultaneously express your displeasure with the group in their handling of the conflict while supporting them as individuals. You must also confront the conflict for what it is—a difference in perception or opinion—and determine the essence of the conflict.

Once the conflict has been defined, you must consider how best to deal with the group or the affected group member.

> **TIP**
>
> The secret to managing dysfunctional conflict successfully is to focus on the issue, not the person(s).

When you are lending support and dealing with the conflict, learn to accept another's position even though it differs from yours.

Choose an appropriate conflict resolution style for its effectiveness in the particular situation.

Conflict Resolution Styles

- **Avoidance:** A nonconfrontational approach to conflict. It ignores or passes over issues by not dealing with them directly and thus denies issues are a problem. It may be the right approach when the differences are too minor or too great to resolve or facing the issue might damage relationships further and create more conflict.
- **Accommodation:** Agreeable, nonassertive approach to conflict, with cooperation sought at the expense of personal or professional goals. Accommodation is often made so as not to create disharmony or damage relationships.
- **Win-lose:** A confrontational, assertive, and aggressive style. This win-lose style is suggested only when rules and regulations or standards have not been upheld by the individual as set forth by

the organization, nurse leader, and/or team. Winning is achieved at all costs, and damage occurs within relationships.
- **Compromise:** An aggressive but cooperative style to conflict. All participants achieve positive results and maintain harmonious relationships.
- **Problem solving:** An assertive and cooperative style to conflict. All participants see their needs as important, openly discuss issues, and look for a mutually beneficial solution.

Seven Steps to Conflict Resolution

1. Schedule a meeting with the group member within 24 to 48 hours to discuss the conflict.
2. Begin the meeting with an acknowledgment and confirmation that a conflict exits.
3. Use "I" statements to avoid blaming or accusations. Encourage the group member to use "I" statements as well.
4. Ask direct questions that require the group member to elaborate about the conflict.
5. Listen carefully to what the group member is saying, and repeat what you are hearing. This is a good way to show you fully understand.
6. Tell the group member what you expect as an outcome based on the discussion of the conflict. Ask the group member what he or she would like from you.
7. Agree to a mutual resolution, and schedule a follow-up meeting.

Facilitating conflict resolution often means dealing with difficult people. Difficult people can be a poor influence on those around them. They are usually negative, constantly complain, and in general are quite irritating. As the facilitator of the group, you will have to learn to accept the group member's behavior and genuinely listen despite the person's seemingly poor attitude.

Lewis-Ford (1993) suggests that the best tactics for handling the difficult person's behavior are to remain calm, lower your voice, determine whether it is the person or the situation that is difficult, and avoid internalizing or taking the behavior personally. Once you are able to assess difficult behaviors, you can take the appropriate action.

Dealing with the People Who Cause Conflict

- **Attackers assert their feelings, thoughts, and ideas forcefully; demand that others listen to what they have to say; and require time and space to ventilate their viewpoint.**
  Action: Address attackers by name, and quietly but firmly ask them to kindly sit down. Listen carefully to what they have to say. Remaining calm throughout the discussion and speaking slowly and deliberately has a quieting and comforting effect.
- **Egotists assert their feelings and thoughts in a self-centered fashion and expect others to listen because they consider themselves an expert on the subject. They will seek to be the center of attention in group settings.**
  Action: Be honest and respectful toward their feelings and thoughts but without allowing yourself to become intimidated by their feelings of superiority. Tap their resources by asking questions, and thank them for their contributions. Be firm, stand your ground, and let them know you are the leader.
- **Sneaks use sarcasm and openly criticize others, say one thing but mean something else, and often set others up for failure.**
  Action: Directly confront sneaks with questions that address their attitude and behaviors. State that you do not approve of their sarcasm and negative attitudes, then suggest positive ways to improve their behavior. Encourage sneaks to transform themselves into team players.
- **Victims, or chronic complainers, have a negative perspective about the world in general. They view the glass as half empty and will act hopeless, defeated, and powerless.**
  Action: Encourage victims to express their negative feelings openly, then ask why they hold this perspective. Mutually seek to improve this perspective by examining the situation. Offer resources and assistance where needed.
- **Negators see the world through their eyes only, and are convinced that *their* way is the right way. They do not trust or respect those in positions of authority.**
  Action: Use a collective approach to deal with negators. Have team members offer ideas, thoughts, and recommendations to solve problems in the presence of negators. Peer pressure along with alternative views will let negators see the light.
- **Superagreeable people seek approval from others. Although they quickly volunteer for a job, they often fail to come through.**

Action: Superagreeable people need a lot of recognition. Acknowledge their efforts and monitor work assignments. Look for timely completion of assignments and reward accordingly.
- **Unresponsive people tend to be withdrawn and keep to themselves. They usually have a flat affect and rarely contribute to team efforts or group process. They are often viewed as the wallflowers of the group.**
Action: Actively engage unresponsive people through open-ended questions to broaden the dialogue and ask for their assistance on a given assignment. Try to assign a team member for social support and peer guidance.

Nurse leaders' success in facilitating the group process while handling difficult people depends on the following abilities:

- Knowledge of one's strengths.
- The capacity to nurture those strengths.
- The ability to work with all personalities and situations.
- The capacity to accept people as they are, *not* as you would like them to be.
- The ability to treat difficult people with the same courteous attention displayed to those who are consistently kind and supportive.

There will be times when difficult people will challenge your leadership, sabotage your change efforts, and hamper your enthusiasm. These efforts should not dissuade your intentions. Keep focused, ask them to join you, and encourage and engage them to work as team players.

Facilitator Responsibilities

Nurse leaders are responsible for the norms that govern the behavior of team members in the group. The facilitator serves as an example to all group members.

Leader Responsibilities

- **To develop a set of moral principles that govern patient care and group process.**
- **To reinforce these moral principles.**

- To build a sense of social responsibility among group members.
- To work willingly with all team members, including their short comings.

As the group norms are translated in the culture of the organization, the nurse leader has the opportunity to promote a "constructive culture based on achievement, self-actualization, encouragement of humanism, and affiliative norms" (McDaniel and Stumpf, 1993, p. 54).

Summary

Nurse leaders can provide the proper environment for facilitation by designing a group atmosphere in which participation and sharing of feelings, thoughts, and ideas are valued. The real work of facilitation is done by group members. The nurse leader serves the crucial role of seeing that the right work gets done at the right time, it flows together harmoniously, and desired outcomes are achieved. This is the true work of a skillful facilitator. The end result is that group members achieve a sense of meaning in their work and a desire to challenge themselves to experience excellence in clinical practice.

References

Conger, J. (1993). The brave new world of leadership training. *Organizational Dynamics, 21*(3), 46–58.

Davis, L., and Cox, R. (1994). Looking through the constructivist lens: The art of creating nursing work groups. *Journal of Professional Nursing, 10*(1), 28–34.

Jeffries, E. (1992). *The heart of leadership: Influencing by design*. Dubuque, IA: Kendall/Hunt Publishing Co.

Lewis-Ford, B. (1993). Management techniques: Coping with difficult people. *Nursing Management, 24*(3), 36–38.

McDaniel, C., and Stumpf, L. (1993). The organizational culture: Implications. *Journal of Nursing Administration, 23*(4), 54–60.

CHAPTER 8

Human Resources Management

> Acceptance of the person requires a tolerance of imperfection. Anybody could lead perfect people—if there were any. But there aren't any perfect people.
>
> ROBERT K. GREENLEAF (1991)

Nurse leaders can help team members reach their full potential once they realize that the ability to help other individuals succeed is at the heart of managing human resources and recognize that the success of their organization depends on the people who work for it. The challenge is not only to help people develop themselves but also to ensure that they do so in a way that is supported and reinforced by the nurse leader. Here, nurse leaders must figure out what it takes to do the job, a task that encompasses defining the job requirements and determining what skills, attitudes, and personnel are needed to do it.

MOBILIZING HUMAN RESOURCES: VISION AND VALUES

1. What are the characteristics and values of team members that would be most supportive toward the organizational or service vision?
2. How can I recruit, motivate, and involve team members in implementing the vision?
3. What are the training and educational requirements for team members to meet the goals and task requirements of the vision?

The responsibility for enhancing and maintaining the work environment rests with nurse leaders. They must continually assess and develop team members' clinical, technical, and interpersonal skills:

- *Clinical skills*—specialized knowledge and judgment used for the diagnosis and treatment of human responses to actual or potential health problems.
- *Technical skills*—specialized knowledge, analytical ability, and facility in the use of the necessary tools and techniques specific to nursing care. Nurse leaders must stand ready to assess, hone, and redirect those skills of assigned team members so they remain confident and competent. Today more than ever before, team members must possess multiple skills and move readily across functional boundaries.
- *Interpersonal skills*—connecting the human side of people to the task requirements of the organization, including tending to human relations: communication, consideration, and cooperation.

> **TIP**
> Nurse leaders have an obligation to match each worker's ability and talents to the needs and requirements of the workplace.

FORGING A PARTNERSHIP

A **partnership** is a desired relationship between two parties seeking to work together toward a common goal. To establish this new relationship, both parties must be willing to conduct a self-assessment—a systematic process of taking stock of those attributes that influence one's effectiveness, success, and happiness. If nurse leaders are truly to manage human resources and forge a partnership with each member of the team, then self-assessment becomes a tool for bridging people and work. Team members will gain a better understanding and appreciation of their work requirements when they understand and empathize with the client or customer. This allows them to shine, ignites their interests, and provides the skills that help them to excel.

An important dimension of human resources management is monitoring personnel productivity, development, and client and customer needs along with achieving the organization's vision, mission, and objectives. These goals can be achieved when nurse leaders are sensitive to the needs of both clients and team members.

> **TIP**
>
> For team members to function with maximum effectiveness, they must understand their relationship with client satisfaction.

MARKET-FOCUSED LEADERSHIP

Nurse leaders are well positioned within the organization to assess the changing needs and desires of both clients and team members, and they have the timing, opportunity, and responsibility. Indeed, nurse leaders' instinctive capacity to empathize with and gain insights from clients and team members is the most important skill they can use to direct nursing care services.

How successful a nurse leader is at assessing the capabilities of the organization to meet patient needs will depend on her market-focused leadership. Unless she makes market focus a personal, strategic priority, she will not meet new market needs or demands. During this time of restructuring and redesign, the organization's ability to survive is dependent on nurse leaders' abilities to:

- Focus on client requirements.
- Develop a strategic effort throughout and within nursing to promote quality.
- Improve and/or revise training requirements to meet the demands of work redesign.
- Promote teamwork.
- Benchmark nursing services and patient care delivery models.

To truly keep your finger on the pulse of market changes,

- Ask clients and team members what they want.
- Provide clients and team members with what they want.
- Treat clients and team members well.
- Make sure clients and team members are satisfied.

How do you begin to deliver services that conform to client and team member requests and requirements? Gouillart and Sturdivant (1994) suggest following a few basic rules:

1. Count on your customers for information, not for insight. You must be able to interpret and solve customer problems.

2. Do not expect great ideas each time you examine a customer study. Sometimes even a small operational shift made from a market-focused perspective can add up to significant improvements.
3. Involve all levels of the organization in the drive to become market focused. For maximum results, be sure the market-focused mind-set permeates the entire organization.

A marketing philosophy can be integrated with nursing practice:

- *Understand your organization's philosophy.* Knowing what the organization stands for—its mission, values, and goals—allows you to focus your leadership and direct resources appropriately.
- *Keep a positive and realistic perspective.* Be sensitive to the resources within the organization—its people and finances. Know the limits and boundaries of your team, and create programs and services accordingly. Keep your plans simple, sensible, and positive. Make sure people know you care, and give personal attention to all those you come in contact with.
- *Do your market research.* Investigate all possibilities; gather the data, research, survey, compare, and contrast. Tap your networks, talking to everyone—locally, regionally, or nationally—who has experience in the areas you are exploring.
- *Create partnerships and networks.* Learn how to build bridges and linkages from the bedside to the boardroom, from inside to outside the organization. Meet with nursing representatives and organization representatives to share ideas, finances, and people. Invest in support services so as not to duplicate programs or services.
- *Plan and set marketing priorities.* Identify marketing goals, and then be ready to evaluate, revise, and adjust your priorities continually. Develop a timeline and stick to it.

Remember that marketing is merely a process of planning and executing the conception, pricing, promotion, and distribution of ideas, goods, and services to create exchanges that satisfy patients, team members, and organization objectives. Nurse leaders who understand the organization's strengths and limitations become instrumental in contributing to the marketing plans and strategies that improve patient care and enhance employee performance.

Understanding the Organization's Purpose and Business

- What does the organization stand for?
- What are the objectives to achieve this?
- How do these objectives affect the organization's marketing plan?
- What type of client mix does this organization serve or desire to serve in the future?
- What type of service should this organization focus on?
- What is the competition doing?

After a careful examination of the organization's vision, mission, and objectives, nurse leaders must move to place the right people into the right work environment in the right job. Fierman (1995) suggests that an organization that allows innovative and radical thinking will create the necessary edge to succeed. By instilling a can-do attitude and the ability to think outside the box, nurse leaders can redesign the workplace to match maverick team members to the vision, values, and core processes of patient care delivery.

How might the best match be made? Develop a checklist that best describes your values and beliefs—for example:

- Nurse autonomy
- Self-directed work teams
- Innovation and creativity
- Informal, nonrigid verbal communication
- Values of quality
- Value of education
- Respect and care for self and others
- Bringing out the best in each individual
- Striving for excellence

Moving People, Making Opportunities

By promoting opportunities for professional development, nurse leaders encourage people to grow, change, and learn. By encouraging personnel to develop a career guide, nurse leaders put the responsibility of orchestrating a nursing career in the hands of the individual. Here are some ways to help team members grow:

1. Create a center listing career opportunities.
2. Designate a bulletin board or a small corner of an office where personnel can be kept informed about the future direction of nursing within the organization.
3. Keep job postings, promotions, and other organization trends easily accessible.
4. Help all individuals to understand that they are responsible for developing their competititve skills. Assist employees to move beyond their job or the organization when the time is right.

Mentoring

One of the key components in a successful career strategy, and second only to education, is **mentoring**. Vance and Olson (1991) define a mentor as a more experienced role model who guides, coaches, and advises the less experienced. Nurse leaders are in an ideal position to become trusted, experienced advisers. They too have learned the ropes from those who have gone before them.

The mentor identifies a younger employee as having potential and takes this chosen person under his or her wing, giving professional advice, pointing out pitfalls, and arranging introductions to the right people. Mentors help with career development and career advancement, provide encouragement and recognition of potential, and foster growth. They add insight when you are lost, fuel to the fire when you are down, and a sounding board when you just need someone to talk to. A mentoring relationship can offer a framework that synthesizes theory, practice, and the role of a leader (Hagenow and McCrea, 1994).

Nurse leaders can create or initiate programs, including mentoring circles, peer mentoring, and one-on-one mentoring in a structured arrangement.

There are ways to make mentoring happen. Here are some points for those seeking a mentor:

1. Assess your needs and those around you.
2. Seek out someone whom you see as a role model.
3. Take a risk and ask for a meeting.
4. Communicate explicitly what you would like from that person.
5. Be active. Do the work; do not just wait around.

Do not assume that a person you seek out to be a mentor, for yourself or your team members, knows how to mentor. He or she may have difficulty in translating knowledge. Cultivate and build that relationship.

Mentoring plays a critical role in the development and grooming of nurse leaders. If you have not been a mentor, now is a time to consider becoming one. Mentorship offers:

- Help to potential nurse leaders to strengthen their confidence, competence, and satisfaction.
- An informal pathway to career growth and development.
- A means of sharing nursing values and cultures.

Networking

Networking is a method that is becoming well known within nursing leadership circles. Networks provide access to crucial information, advice, contacts, and visibility. They also provide avenues for identifying persons who can be helpful and for building relationships and maintaining contacts that are potentially useful. Networks allow you to spin a web that connects you to people who could be useful in your organization, career, and community. They are also more than hearing names; they encompass hearing challenges and solutions too.

Through gestures as simple as a handshake and an exchange of a business card, a network is created. The process may look causal, but it requires some effort to do it right. If you are unsure about how to approach networking, consider the following ways to increase your network base:

- Plan time each week to add to your file names of new contacts.
- Get to know the people on the inside and outside of the organization.
- Look for opportunities to give information as well as get information.
- If you are uneasy about networking, go to meetings or professional nursing organizations that will teach you how to go about it. (Appendix B contains a listing of national nursing organizations.)

To make the most of potential networking encounters, follow these guidelines:

- Focus on what the other person needs, and be prepared.
- Carry business cards. Remember that a business card has two sides. You can use the back side to write a note about a contact, perhaps the date and event that brought you together. This note helps to jog your memory when you are cleaning out your pockets.

- Have a good introduction.
- Make eye contact.
- Shake hands firmly.
- If you have a name tag, wear it on the right for ease of viewing.
- Follow up with a telephone call or a personal note.
- Try e-mail, easy for whipping off a brief note: "I really enjoyed meeting you. When can we meet again?"

Learning how to function in an informal network and to reap the benefits of belonging are important lessons for nurse leaders.

Maintaining Marketability

A personal obstacle that works against nurse leaders is their reluctance to look out for themselves and take credit for their work and ask for what is due. Nurse leaders have been conditioned to contribute behind the scenes and to wait patiently until their worth is recognized. Nurse leaders must overcome this tendency, which is dysfunctional to career development. Instead, they must break out of the mold to advance in their careers and be recognized. Their marketability must be maintained. Koerner (1995) believes that in order for nurse leaders to thrive, not merely survive, in times of unprecedented change, they must have the capacity to see, hear, and develop hardiness.

TIP

Nurse leaders must demonstrate their leadership capability by increasing their visibility, gaining recognition for their work and skill, taking advantage of opportunities, enlarging responsibilities, and getting as close as possible to the centers of power and influence.

Activities for Maintaining Visibility

- **Attend lunchtime seminars.**
- **Work constructively and productively in a network or in relationships with peers, team members, and superiors.**

- Participate in the informal world of organizational life where relationships are based on friendship and loyalty.
- Participate in the formal organization where relationships are based on power, influence, and authority.
- Work with a career counselor on self-assessment.
- Create weekly discussion sessions on the status of health care reform, organization restructuring, or workforce redesign and their implications.
- Establish reference materials to help team members develop plans for professional growth.
- Offer resumé writing and interview workshops or seminars.
- Encourage enrollment or return to school for additional training and education.

THE HIRING PROCESS

As organizations seek to redesign themselves in a reformed health care market, new health positions will be created. It is important that organizations know how to attract the best qualified candidates.

The Resumé

Usually the first contact a job applicant has with a potential employer is the resumé, the marketing tool that reflects the candidate's qualifications on paper (Andrica, 1994). It is an important document and therefore should be clear, concise, and well prepared.

The **resumé** should describe in an easy-to-read format an applicant's education, job experience, and personal and professional attributes. Since the main purpose of the resumé is to obtain an interview, a well-written cover letter accompanying the resumé will often persuade potential employers to give serious consideration to the candidate (King and Sheldon, 1993).

An effective resume uses its professional content, appearance, and organization to invite the reader to pay close attention to it. One page is recommended, unless the candidate has more than five years of relevant work experience. The resumé should be printed professionally on medium-weight white, cream, or buff colored paper, 8½ by 11 inches (Andrica, 1994). Its format is as important as the information it contains (Figure 8.1). Figure 8.2 shows a sample resumé.

Figure 8.1 Putting the Resumé Together

I. Identify your career objective. Formulating a career objective is the first step in the process of creating a resumé. The objective should be specific enough to name a job title in a chosen field.

II. Identify education, experience, and skills.

   A. List educational background.

   B. List relevant experience and skills.

   C. Identify skills and list them using action verbs.

   D. List accomplishments and evidence of skills.

   E. List honors, awards, and certifications.

   F. List professional memberships.

   G. Include job internships, volunteer work, and other relevant extracurricular activities.

III. Format. There are many formats, but the two most common are the chronological and the functional.

   A. The chronological resumé lists education and experience in reverse order (that is, the most recent activity first) with a brief description of each. This format is used when there is:

      1. Relevant work experience

      2. The experience can be related to the current job search

      3. There are no large gaps in the employment history

   B. The functional resumé lists skills with accomplishments. This format is better used if there are:

      1. Changing careers (e.g., from business to nursing)

      2. Gaps in employment history

      3. Lack of relevant experience

WRITING A RESUMÉ

- **Keep the resumé no longer than two to three pages.**
- **Use high-quality bond paper, maintaining generous margins all around.**
- **Be neat, clean, and concise.**
- **Use bulleted points rather than long sentences.**
- **Be truthful on termination dates.**
- **Eliminate nonrelevant personal information.**

FIGURE 8.2 Sample Chronological Resumé

Personal information
Name: _____
Street address: _____
City, state, zip: _____
Home telephone number: _____

Personal objective: _____

Education

Doctoral degree	School: _____	Year graduated: _____
	City, state: _____	
Master's degree	School: _____	Year graduated: _____
	City, state: _____	
Baccalaureate	School: _____	Year graduated: _____
	City, state: _____	
Associate degree	School: _____	Year graduated: _____
	City, state: _____	
Diploma	School: _____	Year graduated: _____
	City, state: _____	

Experience [Beginning with your current or most recent position, describe your professional experience. Be sure to include staff nurse, charge nurse, and other leadership positions.]

From: _____
To: _____
Organization: [Provide the organization's name and location here.]
Title: _____
Responsibilities: _____
Accomplishments: _____

Honors [List honors received within the past five to seven years that reflect achievement in nursing leadership or management.]

Honor: _____ Year received: _____

Professional memberships [List current professional memberships, including any offices you currently hold.]

Organization name: _____
Office position/title: _____

Presentations: _____

Publications: _____

References: Professional and personal references are available on request.

The Cover Letter

When sending a resumé, include a cover letter with

- An introduction
- A job objective
- Current job status
- Request for an interview

This letter is an opportunity to personalize and target the resumé to a particular person in the organization. It should:

- Direct attention to specific skills that may be important to the reader.
- Clearly state why the organization is of interest.
- Open the door for further communication and follow-up.

Figure 8.3 shows a sample letter.

Figure 8.3 Sample Cover Letter

Applicant's address
Applicant phone/fax number
Date of letter

Employer's name and title
Employer's address

Dear [name of person]:

This letter is sent as application for the [title] position advertised in [source and date].

With my ten years of experience in nursing operations, systems, finance, and marketing, I believe I could be an asset to your organization, and I would like to be considered for the position.

I would be pleased to supply additional information and would be happy to meet with you at your convenience.

Thank you for your consideration. I will call you in a few days to discuss the position.

Sincerely,

Signature
[Name typed]

Encl.

To avoid having the doors closed before an interview is granted by a potential employer, consider the following tips:

- Spell the name of the organization correctly.
- Send the letter to the correct address.
- Send the letter to the personnel department with the exact name and title of the person you are contacting. Address the letter "Dear Sir or Madam" when in doubt as to who the hiring authority is.
- Avoid misspelled words and typographical errors.
- Avoid using crumpled paper.
- Avoid poor grammar.
- Remember to enclose the resumé.
- Include a telephone or fax number.
- State that you will follow up with a telephone call in the next few days.

The Interview

An important aspect of managing human resources is finding the right person with the right skills for the right job. The **interview process** offers the opportunity to determine the potential for a good match between the applicant and the job specifications. Interviewing, a structured technique for collecting information from an individual, is a very efficient means of data collection. As the interviewer, the nurse leader becomes the link between the job applicant and the organization (Figure 8.4).

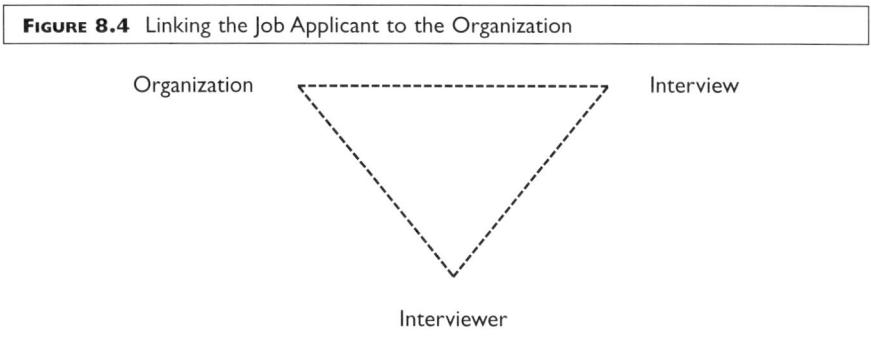

FIGURE 8.4 Linking the Job Applicant to the Organization

Guidelines for an Effective Interview

- **Do your homework.** Know the job requirements, skills, responsibilities, and needed credentials, and prepare a list of questions to ask the job applicant.
- **Explain the job training requirements, salary range, and working conditions.**
- **Discuss the job applicant's strengths, weaknesses, abilities, talents, interests, needs, values, accomplishments, prior work experiences, future job expectations, and short- and long-term goals.**
- **Encourage the job applicant to ask questions. Demonstrate your interest and enthusiasm.**
- **Think of each interview as the first one.**

Use each interview as an opportunity to learn about the position, the organization, and yourself. After the interview, evaluate what you liked and disliked about your interviewing skills and behavior (King, 1993).

Certain character traits may be important to the job in question. During the interview, ask the job applicant to elaborate on those most appropriate—for example:

- Ability to communicate
- Intelligence
- Self-confidence
- Willingness to accept responsibility
- Initiative
- Leadership
- Energy level
- Flexibility
- Interpersonal skills
- Self-knowledge
- Ability to handle conflict
- Competitiveness
- Goal achievement
- Direction

Sample Interview Questions

1. **Common questions**
   - **What are your major strengths?**

- How is your previous work experience relevant to this position?
- Why do you want to work for this organization?
- What are some of your interests outside of work?
2. Personal questions
    - Tell me about yourself.
    - What have been the three most important events [or decisions] of your life?
    - What decisions have you most regretted? Why?
    - What did you like about your previous job? What did you get out of it?
    - What do you judge your major successes [accomplishments] to have been? Your failures? Your major disappointments?
3. Job organization questions
    - Why are you interested in this health care organization?
    - What do you think you will be doing in this job you are applying for?
    - What do you think this job requires, and how do you match these requirements?

Preparing for the Interview. Nurse leaders are required to hire new personnel and promote personnel to new positions, so they must be prepared and results oriented. To get the most out of the interview process:

- Be on time. This means allowing fifteen minutes to focus and center prior to conducting the interview.
- Be relaxed yet attentive, and try to sit next to the applicant.
- Dress appropriately and be well groomed.
- Have questions prepared ahead of time on index cards, and practice reading these in advance of the actual interview.
- Be prepared to listen and to exchange information, keeping in mind that the interview is a conversation between you and the interviewee.
- Be results oriented. Assess and summarize your actions and accomplishments for the interview.

MEETING THE JOB APPLICANT

- Greet the applicant by name, and be prepared to shake hands.
- Look the applicant in the eye, but do not stare.
- Smile and be polite.
- Begin the interview with such openings as: "Tell me about yourself," or "Why are you interested in our organization?"

Ten Questions to Avoid. Interviews are designed to elicit information from the applicant, but there are certain areas that interviewers must avoid:

1. *Children.* Do not ask applicants if they have children, plan to have children, or have child care. Any questions that single out a particular group, such as women, are covered by Title VII of the Civil Rights Act of 1964 and should not be asked. Title VII prohibits discrimination based on race, color, religion, national origin, or sex.
2. *Age.* Do not ask an applicant's age. The Age Discrimination in Employment Act was written to outlaw age discrimination for anyone between the ages of forty and seventy years old.
3. *Disabilities.* Do not ask whether the applicant has a physical or mental disability that would interfere with doing the job. The Americans with Disabilities Act prohibits employers from obtaining this information before a job offer has been made.
4. *Physical characteristics.* Do not ask for such identifying characteristics as height or weight on an application. If it appears on the application form, be sure to cross it out.
5. *Name.* Do not ask female candidates for their maiden name. This question is outlawed under Title VII of the Equal Employment Opportunity Act because it establishes a woman's marital status.
6. *Citizenship.* Do not ask applicants about their citizenship. Be sensitive about national-origin discrimination.
7. *Lawsuits.* Do not ask a job applicant if she or he ever filed a suit or claim against a former employer. Under a variety of federal and state statues, whistle-blowers and workers who have pressed charges against their organizations are protected from retaliation by current and future employers.
8. *Arrest records.* Do not ask applicants about arrest records. An arrest in itself is not proof of anything. What is significant is whether the applicant has ever been convicted of a crime. You *are* entitled to request this information.
9. *Smoking.* Do not ask if a candidate smokes. It is illegal for employers to refuse to hire or to not retain smokers. A more appropriate question is whether the applicant is aware of the organization's regulations and would comply with them.
10. *HIV/AIDS.* Do not ask a job applicant if he or she is HIV positive or has AIDS. These questions are in violation of the disabilities law and could violate state and federal civil right laws.

Red Flags. When conducting an interview, be alert to the following red flags signaling potential problems:

- Sloppy appearance (inappropriate clothing or poor personal hygiene, for example).
- Sloppy preparation of the job application. Note if essential information is missing on the form.
- Limp handshake.
- Lack of confidence and poise, nervousness, an ill-at-ease appearance.
- Lack of interest and enthusiasm; passive and indifferent.
- Inability to express self clearly; poor voice, diction, and grammar.
- Overbearing; overaggressive; conceited "know-it-all" attitude.
- Lack of planning for career; no purpose or goals.
- Lack of tact and courtesy; poor manners.
- Little eye contact.
- Indecisiveness.
- Evasiveness; hedges on unfavorable factors in record or makes excuses.
- Lack of knowledge of field of specialization.
- Being late to the interview without a good reason.
- Asking no questions about the job or position.
- Indefinite responses to questions.
- Cynicism.
- No interest in the vision or mission of the organization.
- Answering questions with only "yes" or "no."
- Uses negative-sounding words or phases (e.g., "only just," "merely").

SUMMARY

Nurse leaders are being challenged to manage human resources more effectively while encouraging a diversity of views and empowering team members to develop their own ideas. Promoting opportunities for personal and professional growth for team members in the organization leads to a commitment to employability. Nurse leaders must appreciate the diversity of human skills and the unpredictability of the human spirit. By fostering a work environment that promotes growth through job training, counseling, mentoring, and networking, nurse leaders recapture those valuable human attributes not only for the individual but for the organization as well. The ability to secure a work environment where individuals flourish while achieving performance criteria and quality outcomes is reflected in the nurse leader's ability to find the best candidate. When the nurse leader has a picture of who the desired candidate is, the interviewing and hiring process can be developed. This process should include those characteristics and competencies the candidate should possess to fulfill the role. The nurse leader must give significant time and thought to interviewing and hiring. Well-constructed questions as well as a careful review of the resumé will allow the nurse leader to select the candidate with the "best fit" for organization and team values.

REFERENCES

Andrica, D. C. (1994). Competing in the new job market: Part I—your resumé. *Nursing Economics, 12*(6), 344–345.

Fierman, J. (1995). Winning ideas from maverick managers. *Fortune, 131*(2), 66–80.

Greenleaf, R. (1991). *Servant leadership.* New York: Paulist Press.

Gouillart, F. J., and Sturdivant (1994, Jan./Feb.). Spend a day in the life of your customer. *Harvard Business Review,* 72, 25.

Hagenow, N., and McCrea, M. (1994). A mentoring relationship: Two viewpoints. *Nursing Management, 25*(12), 42–43.

King, J. A. (1993). *The smart woman's guide to interviewing and salary negotiation.* Hawthorne, NJ: Career Press.

King, J. A., and Sheldon, B. (1993). *The smart woman's guide to resumes and job hunting (2nd edition).* Hawthorne, NJ: Career Press.

Koerner, J. E. (1995). The power of place: Career transformation through stability. *Nursing Science Quarterly, 19*(4), 44–53.

Vance, C. and Olson, R. (1991). Mentorship. In J. J. Fitzpatrick, R. L. Taunton, and A. K. Jacox (Eds.), *Annual review of nursing research,* (pp. 175–200). New York: Springer.

CHAPTER 9

Fostering a Caring Workplace

MARY ELLEN LOREFICE AND DONNA M. COSTELLO-NICKITAS

People won't care how much you know until they know how much you care.
CAVETT ROBERT (1969)

In order for a caring and supportive workplace to exist, two components are essential: strong leadership and effective communication skills. Nurse leaders have an obligation to seek new and different ways to communicate and create a caring and supportive work environment. By using a combination of personal characteristics and therapeutic communication skills, nurse leaders foster an atmosphere of innovation, creativity, and trust. This healthy atmosphere promotes change and provides for healthy communication patterns to emerge.

HEALTHY LEADERS, HEALTHY COMMUNICATION

There will not be healthy communication if the leadership is not healthy. The personal characteristics of a strong leader—integrity, honesty, competence, trust, reliability—cannot be emphasized enough because they can set the tone for effective communication. When these characteristics are present, the nurse leader fosters openness and trust.

> **TIP**
>
> Nurse leaders must demonstrate role model behaviors and actions for all team members to observe.

The way a nurse leader acts in relation to self, team members, and the organization is a constant model for staff and sends a powerful message: that the nurse leader is worth emulating.

Supportive Nurse Leader Behaviors

- **Totally accepting others.**
- **Displaying optimism.**
- **Living an attitude of service.**
- **Communicating a zest for living.**
- **Speaking opinions.**
- **Affirming others.**
- **Showing openness to new ideas.**
- **Accepting compliments.**
- **Displaying a sense of humor.**
- **Being tolerant of others' mistakes.**
- **Being present in the moment.**
- **Accepting your authority.**

Caring and Supportive Leader Behaviors

Kouzes and Posner (1990) found that followers look for leaders who possess the following characteristics: honesty, competence, forward thinking, and inspiration. Strong nurse leaders must also possess an ability to project strength and power, and invite respect.

To capture the attention of team members and encourage them to work toward your desired goals as well as be influenced by you, project an impeccable image. Take the time to evaluate your communication patterns:

- *Verbal language.* Be sure your spoken words are comprehensible, articulate, and conveyed in an intelligent way.
- *Body language.* Physical stature, erect posture, secure hand movements, and a firm stride send an implicit message demanding power and respect.
- *Voice tone.* Calm, quiet talk leads to warmth and approachability.

It is important that team members feel comfortable with their leader. They can become empowered more easily with a nurse leader with whom they feel they can be themselves.

BEING TRUSTWORTHY AND RELIABLE

- *Congruity and constancy.* Walk the walk and talk the talk. There is a commitment to do what is said. Follow-through is important to model; it shapes the work environment and makes a difference whether trust can be promoted.
- *Listening.* Give full attention to the person with whom you are speaking. Team members will more likely engage in conversation when they believe they will be heard. Listen with an open mind, and keep personal prejudices, feelings, and attitudes in check as you concentrate on the message being given.
- *Self-awareness.* Viewing oneself objectively is essential in order to be a good listener. "Owning one's own stuff" is a difficult task. The ability to look inward instead of automatically blaming others affords the opportunity for true emotional growth and is a reflection of maturity. Listening and reflecting on your own behavior is different from listening and just reflecting on someone else's behavior.

Nurse leaders need to be able to speak to team members without making them feel disempowered. To guide and direct team members effectively, nurse leaders must clearly hear the voices and needs of those around them. This requires attentive and empathic listening. Try to put yourself in the place of the person who is talking. Shed your point of view momentarily and take theirs, listening not just with your ears but with your heart. Attentive and empathic listening promotes healthy communication, with both sender and receiver showing genuine interest without interrupting (Navarra, Lipkowitz, and Navarra, 1990).

Nurse leaders have a responsibility to create an atmosphere of support, one that promotes a safe and trusting relationship between leader and team members. First and foremost, nurse leaders must be calm, in control, and approachable. When they are open, warm, and trustworthy, they are modeling respectful behavior.

MODELING RESPECTFUL BEHAVIOR

- Be consistent and act positive.
- Be a good role model by setting an example. Stay calm. People will avoid communicating with someone they perceive as out of control, closed-minded, or distant.

- Treat everyone you meet as though he or she is the most important person you will meet that day.
- Learn the art of giving sincere compliments. People really do care what you think and appreciate your kind comments.

> **TIP**
> Nurse leaders need to be able to speak to staff members without making them feel disempowered.

How to Promote Positive Interaction

- Hear what team members have to say. *Negative:* "Why can't you ..." *Positive:* "What if we ..."
- Avoid negative language and behavior. *Negative:* "She always says ..." *Positive:* "I've heard her say ..."
- Take team members' suggestions and ideas seriously. *Negative:* "We must do it this way." *Positive:* "That's a good idea to consider."

Understanding Communication

Effective communication is an essential component for fostering a caring, supportive workplace. Nurse leaders need to be able communicators to work effectively with staff and make changes within the health care system.

Communication is something we do every day of our lives—and something we have to do in order to survive. It is an expression of ourselves and our individuality. Our capacity to understand ourselves and others and the way we communicate is our individual stamp. It is how we connect our selves to the world, whether we are isolated or feel part of something.

> **TIP**
> Because good communication affects every facet of our lives, it is important to consider how you speak, gesture, and come across, and whether you connect with others.

Communication is a way to be in touch, be joined, give, part, inform, say, and transfer ideas, feelings, and thoughts.

Communication can be seen as a risk, but the risks are reasonable when you have learned some of the techniques that enhance communication. When looking at who says what to whom with what effect, examine the following aspects of communication: the message and the audience.

The Message

The ability of nurse leaders to organize and phrase their messages skillfully determines much of the effectiveness in influencing team members' attitudes and behaviors. It is important to consider the nature of the material that is being presented:

- Is it logical?
- Is it emotional?
- Is it political?
- Is it economical?

The language used to communicate is as important as the way the message is communicated. The words and phrases must be directed at the level of the listener and must be comprehensible. Select words and phrases free of hidden meanings, and be sure the message is clear and contains no insults that might contribute to a communication breakdown. When preparing to send a message, be:

- Careful and thoughtful about words and phrases.
- Attentive to the receiver or audience needs.
- Familiar with barriers to communication (values, beliefs, cultural, and gender differences).

The Audience

Team members are the audience for nurse leader messages. Therefore, it is essential to understand the variety of influences that may affect how the audience hears and interprets the message:

- Personal values and beliefs
- Age
- Education
- Cultural, religious, and ethnic

- Gender
- Self-concept or self-esteem

Being aware of how these influences may distort or otherwise hamper communication, nurse leaders must seek to remain objective and not view any resistance as personal.

Becoming an Effective Communicator

Happiness and success in life often depend on being a good communicator. People who have the most difficulty in life are often those most in need of communication but do not know how to be heard. For example, a person who is doing something self-destructive such as screaming and assuming he or she is being victimized by someone needs to learn to communicate more effectively. This presenting style is so negative that it invites negative communication, not the calm, warm approachability that is needed. This person needs to improve communication skills and needs someone who will listen.

How to Become an Effective Communicator

- *Be sensitive.* Stay in tune on a variety of levels to listeners' needs.
- *Be a team player.* Consider the larger group, and be able to determine what they want by what they are saying.
- *Be focused.* At the end of each conversation, make note of the result and any follow-up that might be needed.
- *Be clear.* Make the message clear and concise; eliminate excess verbiage.
- *Be respectful.* Treat others with a sense of equality despite differences.
- *Be warm and friendly.* A listener who feels comfortable and at ease comes across better and feels better about the communicator.
- *Be dynamic.* A dynamic communicator is perceived as assertive and empathic, and connects with the listener. A dynamic communicator is listened to more often.
- *Be reliable.* Know your facts; be dependable, predictable, and consistent.
- *Be courteous.* Politeness counts.

- *Be positive.* A positive attitude makes all the difference in the success of the communication's being transmitted and eliciting change.
- *Be enthusiastic.* Make the connection and commitment to communicate with energy and effort.
- *Be credible.* Remember to remain honest and true about your motives. Credibility matters whether one's communication is acknowledged or not.

To be effective, nurse leaders must have a good grasp of communication techniques that foster a supportive workplace:

- *Read the signals.* Examine facial expressions and body language. Excessive movements indicate some kind of stress reaction. Look at the consistency between what is said and what the body and voice are actually saying.
- *Demonstrate concern and help.* Let the listener know immediately through your words, tone, actions, and body language that you are there to help her or him regardless of your differences or the nature of the problem or issue at hand.
- *Use stock phases.* Develop a list of statements to rely on in awkward or difficult situations. These stock statements can help to relieve tension and stress.
- *Remain alert and sensitive.* Be aware of and recognize the other person's emotional well-being. Having insight about where a person is coming from emotionally is invaluable.
- *Tone it up or down.* How you say what you say is critical. Just about anything can be said to someone and not be offensive if the tone of the voice is warm, caring, and concerned.
- *Acknowledge your mistakes.* Modeling openness and the acceptability of making and admitting an error is a sign of emotional security. No one is perfect. It is unreasonable for leaders to be rigid and unaccepting of their own errors.
- *Know your boundaries.* When conducting a conversation with a team member, remember to recognize the delicate border that exists between ideal communication and those things that are rightfully private.
- *Provide for a caring environment.* Set up the condition of trust where help can be given and received. A willingness to work with someone affects what you say and sends that caring message to those you are trying to reach. It makes for the understanding and solutions of problems when emotionally there is a safe atmosphere.

- *Use mock staffing.* Switch roles with a team member to gather insight into how that person could work more effectively. This is a non-threatening way to solve problems that may be frustrating. These sessions can increase awareness about how explanations can be improved.
- *Restate to be sure.* Repeat the description of the problem or point presented. By taking the time to restate what was said, you eliminate incorrect information from being inferred.
- *Always seek to clarify.* Take time and make the effort to go over the meaning of what is said. For example, you might say, "I'm not sure what you mean" or "What you mean is . . ."
- *Do not assume prior knowledge.* Try to go into an interaction with an open mind, and put your preconceived ideas aside. Listen as if you have never heard anything about the situation before.
- *Establish chronological order.* Find out exactly what has happened and the exact order of the events. Knowing when things occurred will help in establishing order out of chaos.
- *Remain focused.* Give your attention to the other person's concern by acknowledging it verbally. A small gesture such as this can be very powerful when communicating.
- *Seek to understand the other person.* By trying to understand fully another's point of view, you create a strategy that can work for both parties.
- *Maintain a reality base.* Make sure you are dealing with the facts when communicating. Be realistic and attempt to make reasonable requests.
- *Express healthy skepticism.* This helps to deal with the natural tendency to exaggerate and stretch issues when communicating under stress.
- *Translate.* Try to identify the real issues. Lay them on the table when the content of a conversation is full of emotion.
- *Assess progress.* Ask questions, look at the overall picture, and point to the reality. State what you hear and see gained through your line of questioning.
- *Turn to your third ear.* Listen for hints of the real issue, which is not necessarily the presenting problem. By listening carefully, you may be able to detect the real concern through the content, body language, and expression of the person relaying the problem.
- *Summarize.* After listening and strategizing, summarize the plans. State the important points and highlight the next course of action.
- *Offer guidance.* This is an art form that requires getting through the natural resistance and the need to be heard.
- *Be open and refrain from being judgmental.* Do not expect everyone to hold the same values or perspectives as you do. Be sensitive to differences.

Problem Solving

All nurse leaders eventually must cope with people who are difficult to deal with.

> **TIP**
>
> Nurse leaders are expected to be experts at human relations and problem solving.

Obviously, not every solution undertaken will be the correct one. However, the manner and attitude in which a nurse leader approaches a problem will be remembered. Therefore, avoid negative or "can't-do" attitudes.

There will always be issues, difficult personalities, and negative behavior when problems emerge, and nurse leaders must be prepared. Expect resistance as team members are asked to conform to new structures and designs of the organization.

Dealing with Resistance to Change

1. You cannot control the outcome of the decision. All you can do is control the decision-making process.
2. Start the decision-making process by identifying your wants, needs, and outcomes. Be sure to write them down.
3. Rank the order of your desires and outcomes. If you spot contradictory needs, ask yourself, "Which would I choose?"
4. Gather all the information necessary to make the decision. Look at the alternatives, consequences, advantages, and disadvantages. Do not let emotions interfere with this process. Be as objective as possible.
5. Determine how much of a risk you are willing to take. Once you have done this, consider the alternatives:
   - Choose the safest alternative—the one that cannot fail.
   - Pick the option with the best odds of success.
   - Select the alternative with the most desirable outcome, despite the risk.
6. Eliminate any option that might present a loss you will not be able to live with, despite high odds for its success. Picture how you will deal with negative consequences.

Problem-Solving Communication Skills

1. When confronted with a problem, respond promptly. Allow the other person to express his or her feelings fully. Then acknowledge your awareness of the situation, describe what you see and hear, reveal what you think and feel, and say what you want.
2. Stay cool and calm. Treat everyone with kindness regardless of how people treat you. Be direct but likable and polite. It is difficult to treat a thoughtful person thoughtlessly.
3. Observe for subtle cues. Pick up the mood and attitude of the other person. Do not take a position, deal with a need. Find out what motivates the person so you can offer alternative ways of solving the problem. Chances are the person confronting you has simply adopted the most obvious solution, so move from *what* the person wants to *why* the person wants it.
4. Make sure you are the appropriate person to handle the problem. Look at the chain of command. It is essential that both nurse leader and team members respect and adhere to the appropriate channels for problem resolution. Not following the chain of command often alienates many people by making them feel overlooked or not given the appropriate respect that comes with their title.
5. Delve beyond the surface. Be sure to explore beyond the presented problem. Look for hidden issues by asking probing questions.
6. Allow for anger to surface. Give permission for anger to be expressed and demonstrate concern. Generally, after a minute or two, the anger will subside and the person will tend to back down.
7. Seek clarification. Once you have heard the facts, it is best to clarify what has been said so far—for example, "Let me repeat what you've said so far …"
8. Do not assume someone is against you unless you hear an accusation. Avoid messages that come via the grapevine.
9. Never presume anything. Do not presume you understand another's feelings or perceptions. If you have not actually experienced what is being described as the problem, it might be difficult to offer the right solution. Spend time listening and exploring the problem rather than rushing toward a solution.
10. Make the implicit explicit. Be sure to articulate your ideas, thoughts, and feelings as well as understanding the ideas,

thoughts, and feelings of those around you. It takes courage and creates respect when the real issues are put forth.
11. Avoid generalities. Be specific; get details. This takes time and effort but is well worth it. Specific exploration is an indication of a richer dialogue.
12. Speak for yourself and no one else. Do not speak or address an area that is not under your jurisdiction. Feel free to offer your opinion, but do not speak on behalf of the organization or team members unless called on to do so.
13. Show flexibility. A change in response to a reasonable request or argument is always appropriate. It is the rigidity or inflexibility on the part of the leader that is not.
14. Use *us* or *we* instead of *you*. You avoid polarizing the team and create a unified atmosphere.
15. Do not push a person beyond his or her limits. In this situation, both parties will come away with lowered self-esteem. Seek always to bring out the best in a person.
16. Find common ground, and use feedback for closure. Before ending any communication, identify common issues or concerns and, seek to clarify decisions or outcomes.
17. When appropriate, put agreements in writing. In this way, both parties clarify their intent and formalize their actions.

Rekindling the Workplace

To improve communication and recharge the energy and efforts between the nurse leader and team members, create a workplace where people look forward to coming to work (Lutz, 1990). Begin with creating an environment where:

- People really trust and respect one another.
- Behavior is recognized that supports the best interests of the organization while respecting individuality.
- Failure without condemnation is allowed.

By creating a workplace that gives people hope for a better future, nurse leaders instill a spirit of courage, compassion, and commitment. Figure 9.1 provides key strategies that enable nurse leaders to foster commitment and caring.

> **FIGURE 9.1** Strategies to Foster Commitment

1. Monitor the energy thermostat.

   a. Look for the presence of stress:
      - High levels of tension.
      - High levels of criticism within the unit, service, and/or department.
      - Anger and bad feelings between team members.

   b. Find out what is wrong and fix it.
      - Play detective and find out what is on the mind of team members. Talk to each member personally if you have to uncover the cause of the stress.
      - Find out what motivates every team member, and make an effort to support it.
      - Find out the barriers, and remove them.

   c. Recharge team members quickly when the thermostat reads low.
      - Give a wake-up call: serve coffee, tea, or another favorite beverage. By providing small nourishment, you are sending a message that you care.
      - Provide minichallenges with small but attainable goals.
      - Communicate constantly and recognize achievements. Give on-the-spot praise and then continually.
      - Make success a daily occurrence. Show how desired outcomes can happen.
      - Develop a recognition program. Identify the champion—the person who goes the extra mile. The recognition can be as simple as a written note or a computer-printed acknowledgment. It could be more elaborate, such as designating an Employee of the Month (or Year). Recognition programs are so effective because of the ability of the nurse manager to make the rewards worthwhile (e.g., a prime parking space next to the building entrance or tickets to the theater or ballet). The reward is seen as a valued prize and something the employee can be proud to have received.

   The bottom line to energy maintenance is that when things are good, make them better; when things are down, give team members a jump start. Team members who feel productive want to come to work. By taking the time to monitor the energy level of your team, you show a commitment to their health and well-being.

2. Share the work, show the spirit, and put team members in charge.

   a. Keep team members informed of ongoing changes within the unit, service, and/or department. Take the time to put the information into perspective so that each team member can relate the change to his or her job duties. Put top-down edicts into digestible terms that help team members fix a problem.

FIGURE 9.1 *continued*

    b. Help team members to understand the big picture and think beyond their own situation. Try to emphasize a commitment to the entire organization. Give the most accurate information possible, then foster self-investment and self-development. Team members' finding the answer to problems will keep morale high.

    c. Make sure everyone brings something to the table. As a leader you can help team members by playing matchmaker and putting members of the team together.

    d. Light the fire and watch what happens.

3. Select workplace projects carefully. Select a few projects that team members can easily accomplish. By achieving desired outcomes and racking up some winning points, team members experience a surge in energy. When the selected projects are visible and important and they benefit patients' care, there is a recognition that team members are vital to the organization. Small projects provide ample opportunities for team members to express their opinions as well as review and revise policies, procedures, and standards of practice as needed.

SUMMARY

The challenge for nurse leaders is to foster an environment that is positive, creative, and caring while maximizing resources and streamlining costs. A positive work environment is essential for job satisfaction, good performance, and high motivation. Therefore, nurse leaders are responsible for creating a system that motivates employees to excel (Shaughnessy, 1990). A trusting environment is built by encouraging team members to share their issues and together resolve their concerns. Communication is an important component of fostering a caring and supportive workplace. Particular emphasis must be placed on the significance and relationship of communication and leadership. Nurse leaders are instrumental in setting the structure for communication—implicit and explicit. A nurse leader with the ability to examine her own behavior objectively sets the stage for a caring and supportive workplace to exist.

REFERENCES

Kouzes, J. and Posner, B. (1990). *The leadership challenge.* San Francisco: Jossey-Bass.

Lutz, S. (1990). Hospitals stretch their creativity to motivate workers. *Modern Health Care,* 20–24, 32–33.

Navarra, T., Lipkowitz, M., and Navarra, J. (1990). *Therapeutic communication*. Thorofare, NJ: Slack, Inc.

Robert, C. (1969). *Human engineering and motivation*. West Nyack, NY: Parker Pub. Co.

Shaughnessy, M. K. (1990). Motivating the staff toward job enrichment. *Today's OR Nurse*, 19–23.

Chapter 10

Time Management

The hours of folly are measured by the clock, but of wisdom no clock can measure.
WILLIAM BLAKE (1790)

A majority of the work nurse leaders do on a daily basis is planning. However, no amount of planning will be successful without the key element of organization. To orchestrate a planning system or framework, nurse leaders must have a basic understanding of what organization is—time management at its best—and what it requires. Focusing on your important goals or tasks can lead to personal and organization effectiveness.

By choosing the most important tasks and letting go of the rest you can solve your time problems. **Time management** is an ongoing process of clarifying your visions and values, identifying long-range goals, and organizing a daily, weekly, and monthly calendar to balance your physical, mental, spiritual, and social-emotional activities.

> **TIP**
>
> A **keeping-track** process is a time management plan that will reduce the number of crises in your life and will lead to increased personal satisfaction, effectiveness, and results.

GETTING STARTED

Before you learn how to get organized, think about how you can break down tasks or large projects into smaller ones. Ask yourself the following questions:

- What should I do first?
- What is most important?

- What are my priorities?
- What are my time problems?

As you assess your situation, be specific, and write down your answers. Start the process by conducting a personal inventory of your activities. Write down your activities in 15- to 30-minute intervals. Keep this time log for one week to monitor what you are doing on any given day (see Figure 10.1). At the end of the week, analyze the time log to identify your key tasks and goals. By studying what you have done versus what you want to do, you refocus your energies to work systematically and progressively toward achieving your goals.

FIGURE 10.1 A Daily Time Log

Time	
6:00 A.M.	_____
6:30	_____
7:00	_____
7:30	_____
8:00	_____
8:30	_____
9:00	_____
9:30	_____
10:00	_____
10:30	_____
11:00	_____
11:30	_____
12:00 P.M.	_____
12:30	_____
1:00	_____
1:30	_____
2:00	_____
2:30	_____
3:00	_____
3:30	_____
4:00	_____
4:30	_____
5:00	_____
5:30	_____

Staying Focused

Once you have made a personal commitment to get organized and disciplined, you must become centered or focused. This will provide you with initial insight into your situation. Allow yourself the time to consider what you want to accomplish. When you begin to think over your goals or tasks freely and openly, ideas will begin to flow spontaneously. This brainstorming is one of the most important time-saving techniques.

Brainstorming allows the brain to let go and produce a flood of thoughts and ideas. The purpose of brainstorming is to break down your organized goals or tasks into smaller bite-sized parts. This strategy allows you to take one bite at a time rather than attempting to achieve the whole goal all at once.

An effective way to focus on what you want to be or do is to create a personal mission statement that provides overall direction and gives purpose and meaning to your life. As a nurse leader you may want to begin by creating a mission statement that reflects your commitment to your patients and team members.

A Sample Mission Statement

"I am committed to providing my patients and team members with high-quality and responsive leadership and creating a caring and productive working environment. I will seek to be honest, courteous, and professional at all times. I will be sensitive to patients' and team members' needs and remain dedicated to their satisfaction."

Once your personal mission statement is formulated, identify your goals. Start by making a list of your goals (see Figure 10.2). Select any goal that you want to be or do: character strengths you want to have, qualities you want to develop, goals you want to accomplish, contributions you want to make.

Find a quiet place where you will not be interrupted. Pick up a pencil (or use the computer), focus on your goal, and start writing the bits and pieces of anything that comes to mind. Just get it written. There is no right or wrong answer or specific order to making this list. Keep brainstorming the list until each goal is broken down into a smaller and smaller unit (see Figure 10.3).

The trick is to think that you can manage or achieve whatever it is you set out to do. Goals are the outcomes of what you want to achieve personally or professionally. You must be able to say, "That's it. I can do that."

CHAPTER 10 TIME MANAGEMENT

FIGURE 10.2 Goal List

1. <u>Get promoted to a leadership position. (sample goal)</u>
2. _____
3. _____
4. _____
5. _____
6. _____
7. _____
8. _____
9. _____
10. _____

COMPONENTS OF GOAL FORMULATION

- **Be clear and attainable.**
- **Be measurable.**
- **Be realistic.**
- **Have a reasonable deadline.**
- **Review and revise as necessary.**

If you take the time to brainstorm first, you have a real opportunity to think over every possible plan.

FIGURE 10.3 Sample Goal: Bite-Sized Units

Get promoted to a leadership position.
- Check career opportunities within the organization or professional journals.
- Talk to employment agencies and headhunters.
- Talk with friends and professional colleagues.
- Rewrite my resumé; make a draft.
- Set up appointments for job interviews.

By breaking goals into smaller units, you will not overlook anything, and the goal or goals will seem less overwhelming. Bite-sized brainstorming is easy and fun. It can help you turn your goals into action plans that are organized and achievable.

Be sure to create an action plan for each identified goal. This will help to further the thinking process and provide a logical step-by-step plan to achieve the goal.

> **TIP**
>
> Begin each day with a clear understanding of your desired goal or direction. Create it mentally, set priorities, and start planning.

CREATING AN ACTION PLAN

1. *Create a mental picture.* Draw and visualize in your mind the fulfillment of your goal. When you achieve your goal, what will it look like? What will it feel like?
2. *Communicate your goal.* Tell those you love and care for what you are striving for.
3. *Commit your resources.* Invest the time, money, and energy to fulfill your goal.
4. *Create a contract.* Draw up a contract with yourself. Identify the steps you will take toward achieving this goal. Write down a completion date for this goal.
5. *Celebrate your goal achievement.* Plan some rewards along the way. Think about how you will celebrate and with whom when the goal is finally accomplished.

ONE STEP AT A TIME

Once your goal list is fully developed, take the time to organize the goals or tasks into similar groups. By taking it slowly and one step at a time, you can create a formula to organize similar groups or categories.

> **TIP**
>
> Grouping like things together saves time, keeps you focused, and builds momentum. Try dividing your tasks or goals into categories—for example, things to do, things to write, people to call, places to visit.

Take the item from each of the four categories of "to do" and write them down. Recording your to-do items into a small notebook of some kind allows you to monitor the things you want to do.

A notebook becomes your mini–filing cabinet (see Figure 10.4). Learning the discipline of writing things down will help in the planning process. It is a great time-saving device and does not force you to commit everything to memory. A notebook allows you the freedom to be creative while not losing sight of your ideas.

FIGURE 10.4 Sample Mini–Filing Cabinet for Notebook

To Do
- Read newspapers and professional journals.
- Read job postings in the nurse recruiter's office.

To Write
- Outline resumé.
- Make a draft resumé.
- Write and print final copy of resumé on computer.

To Call
- Call Mary Ellen for lunch and talk about promotion.
- Call Ms. Nelson re: organization opportunities.

To Visit
- Visit job fairs.
- Visit health-related employment agencies.
- Attend a professional convention or conference.

FIGURE 10.5 Sample Calendar

Monday

7:30 A.M.	Breakfast meeting with vice president of nursing
8:30 A.M.	Staff meeting
10:00 A.M.	Write the vacation/holiday schedule
11:30 A.M.	Attend marketing conference

Living by the Calendar

As you get used to writing your ideas and to-do lists in a notebook, try recording your scheduled appointments on a calendar. In this way, structured time is automatically built into your day. You thus block time on your calendar for activities that involve your personal deadlines. These are deadlines for which no one but you says, "It must be done today." Be smart and learn to write your deadlines on your calendar (see Figure 10.5).

As you learn to plan blocks of time on your calendar, you will move closer toward achieving the assigned task. By learning to write down what needs to be done on a given day, you also create a mental map that helps push the thinking into doing.

> **TIP**
>
> Commit yourself to organizing and writing your key activities down. Set up a regular time to do it.

Effectively living with a calendar means having it available. This means keeping the calendar with you at all times. Otherwise you have to remember dates, places, people, and things, and then translate these into time slots.

The calendar is a tool for keeping track of your life, not controlling your life. Use it to help you find the right balance in setting goals.

The Daily List

The calendar should be a springboard into composing a daily to-do list. Think of the calendar as the whole pie and the daily list as slices. As you glance at the calendar and examine the whole day of projected activities, break down those activities into those things you want to remember to do. In this way you avoid being overwhelmed by taking on too many slices or activities at once. The daily list allows you to decide what to do by setting your priorities.

> **TIP**
>
> By writing down everything you need to accomplish in a day, you can develop a list of priorities.

CATEGORIZING PRIORITIES

1. *The critical:* **A** list activities, essential and due today.
2. *The intermediates:* **B** list activities, important to do today if possible.
3. *The not urgent:* **C** list activities, which can be delayed if necessary.

Lakein (1973) claims that most people spend 80 percent of their time doing C activities and only 20 percent on A activities. Yet it is the A activities that truly make a difference. To achieve maximum results, select a few vital tasks from your daily list—usually not more than two. This will allow you to use 20 percent your time and energy and get 80 percent on your return. The most important task is to define what you want and what you value. By knowing what you value, you can add the critical or high-priority activities to your daily list.

As you begin selecting from the high-priority tasks, consider the best time to accomplish these tasks. Understanding your own biological clock will help in planning the best use of your time. Do you know the peaks and valleys of your energy cycle on a given day? Are you a "day person" or a "night person"? An "early bird" or "night owl"? By knowing your peak energy cycle or prime time period, you can select the time block to accomplish those critical A priority tasks. Work smarter, not harder, during your prime time. Leave the C list (not urgent) tasks for your more sluggish and less productive time period.

> **TIP**
>
> Take a look at your calendar and rearrange your to-do list to reflect your biological clock.

Ulrich (1985) suggests that once you have assessed your energy clock, divide physical and mental activities into the following categories:

High-Peak Activities

- Build relationships within the organization.
- Write a personal mission statement.
- Develop long-range planning.
- Begin an exercise program.
- Solve problems.
- Make decisions.
- Start a project.
- Attend important meetings.
- Develop new ideas.
- Write meaningful correspondence.

Low-Peak Activities

- Complete routine tasks.
- Complete performance evaluations.
- Organize your in-box or desk.
- Initiate and return phone calls.
- Prepare tomorrow's to-do list.

Covey (1989) believes that the essence of time management is to organize and execute around priorities. Thus, the challenge is to organize around what is truly important. The key is to schedule your priorities in peak times throughout the day. Remember that 80 percent of the desired results will come from 20 percent of the activities. Therefore, focus your attention on the important activities.

PUSHING PRIORITIES, ELIMINATING WASTERS

To achieve maximum results, prioritize your goals so every action you perform takes you closer to achieving them.

> **TIP**
> Determine the daily priorities, and write the action steps for your goals each day.

There will be occasions when the best-laid plans may crumble, but remember:

- Keep a steady pace.
- Expect the unexpected as the day unfolds.
- Know how and when to delegate.
- Learn to say no.

Saying no to others and yes to yourself is not an easy task. The word *no* is a very effective time management tool, but it will not always win friends and influence people. The best situation is to make a case that you need time to think about it and will get back with a response in twenty-four hours. By postponing your reply, you collect your thoughts. You can respond to the request with an alternate plan or with a possible substitute in your place. This frees up your guilt and leaves the caller with an alternate solution. Saying no at first is hard. It will get easier when you develop an ability to say no to nonessential demands.

Consider the following list of time wasters and ask yourself how you can reduce or even eliminate them (Mackenzie, 1972):

- Telephone interruptions
- Crisis management, shifting priorities
- Lack of objectives, priorities, and planning
- Drop-in visitors
- Ineffective delegation
- Attempting too much
- Meetings
- Personal disorganization, cluttered desk
- Wasting other people's time
- Lack of self-discipline

BECOMING A TIME SAVER

You control your own time. Become a time saver by applying the following measures to your daily leadership activities.

Delegate

When in doubt, delegate everything except those activities that require your personal attention.

> **TIP**
>
> Delegate intelligently and when you need more time for your work.

Delegation not only saves you time but also develops self-esteem and confidence in those around you. When you learn to delegate effectively, your team members learn to think for themselves and gain a sense of ownership in the results. Effective delegation takes patience and follow-up. However, in the long run, your job gets easier and team members become more productive.

How to Delegate Effectively

1. Try to match the task to the team member.
2. **Make a list of responsibilities you could delegate and the team members you could delegate to or train to be responsible in leadership or patient care areas. Determine what is needed to start the process of delegation.**
3. **Consider the team member's current work assignment.** Go over the assignment carefully to be sure the person understands the task requirements and outcomes. Allow the team member the opportunity to ask questions. Be sure to allow for plenty of autonomy, time, and authority. Convey a feeling of confidence toward the team member as she assumes this new responsibility. Then mutually agree upon a date and time for the task to be accomplished.
4. Be sure to say, "Thanks for being my time saver."

Prioritize Activities

Learn to plan and organize your activities from most important to least important. Each one minute of planning gives you approximately four minutes of extra time, so begin right now. Determine what it is you want, where you want to be at some point in time, and how to get there. Establish target dates for your small, medium, and large goals or projects. Be very specific when these goals will be achieved. Mark the calendar and note your progress. Reenergize each day by planning for what you need to do the next day. Create your to-do list the night before.

First Things First

- *Deal with interruptions openly and directly.* Refuse to do the unimportant. Forget the unnecessary. Ignore the irrelevant. Develop a personal philosophy about time. Try to relate your priorities to your daily calendar. This task is not easy, but you must learn to say no. Be positive and assertive as you communicate why you cannot do something. Offer some alternatives or other potential resources.
- *Improve telephone communications.* When possible, automate and use voice mail. If voice mail is not an option, have someone else screen all your calls. When returning calls, set aside a block of time when you are free and will not be distracted.
- *Make the most of meeting time.* Go prepared with an agenda. Encourage the chair to start and end the meeting on time. Or suggest that the last person to arrive at the meeting brings the coffee to the next session. Another possibility is to schedule the meeting at least one hour before lunch or one hour before the end of the day. This time block will encourage participants to work efficiently and move the agenda along.
- *Reduce the paper trail.* Do not allow your memos, letters, and reports to pile up. Pick each paper up only once and then dispatch it. Pass it or assign it to someone else. Make a decision while the paper is still in your hand what will be done with it. If no decision or response is needed, then discard it. Save paper and time by responding to memos on the bottom of the page. Keep it short and simple. Eventually people will get the message that the paper trail needs to be reduced.
- *Block time for selected activities.* Set a date and time to accomplish special projects. Gather all the necessary data before you start the project, close the door to your office and post a "do not disturb" sign, and have telephone calls held until your time is up.
- *Clean the clutter from your desk.* Take the time and make the effort to remove everything from the top of your desk. As you go through each item, ask yourself, "Is this worth saving?". Based on your decision, discard or file the item. As you reorganize your desk, put essential items in an easy-to-reach spot back into your desk. Place less frequently used items in a C box or file. Then create an A box or file for important papers and projects. These items can be reviewed every thirty days and dispatched as necessary. A clear desk and a neat office are symbols of control over your life and time.

Making Tracks

As a nurse leader you are not only responsible for your own self-imposed time requirements but must respond to organization time requirements as well. These requirements include the time devoted toward meeting the needs and demands made by team members, peers and colleagues, and the boss. Oncken and Wass (1990) call these time commitments **management time.**

To facilitate meeting the demands made on your management time, review your requirements to meet the needs of your team, peer, and boss.

Team Member Time

As a nurse leader you have a certain obligation to set aside time to meet the daily requests and requirements of team members. This time often will include training, coaching, counseling, and support and recognition. The key to managing the timing and content of time spent with team members is to plan ahead as often as possible. Establish a mutual place, time, and activity. This will allow you to minimize surprises or crises should they arise. Nevertheless, always be prepared for the unexpected, and make a quick decision whether the issue or item should be dealt with or delayed.

You are in control of how and when you use your time. When you give away your power to control your allotted time, you will pay the price in other ways: Your identified daily goals or tasks are delayed and left incomplete. Be diligent and responsive to team members but never at the expense of postponing a deadline or commitment. Learn to stop, listen, and respond with a simple, "I hear and understand what you are saying but cannot respond at this moment. I will get back to you." This response allows your team members to know that you care but are not available now to handle their request.

Peer and Colleague Time

All nurse leaders at one time or another will be called on by a peer or colleague for a special request or consultation. These requests for **peer and colleague time** are important and should not be denied. When possible, try to assess their urgency and prioritize an appropriate response.

If your assistance is not readily available, say so, then offer a reasonable time frame or another alternative. Never leave peers or colleagues unattended. After all, you may need their assistance sometime. Peer-imposed time does offer many opportunities for networking and peer support. Be open, flexible, and available, but do not forget the daily personal and other professional obligations.

Boss Time

Understand the difference in meeting the obligations demanded by team members and peers and those imposed by the boss. At no time can nurse leaders ignore or deny those requests the boss requires. **Boss time** is generally expected as a reasonable component of the nurse leader's job. When the request is made, be sure you know enough to get involved and whether you can easily accommodate the time element. If not, be prepared to make an on-the-spot decision not to accept the request and state the reason. You must be alert and responsive to accommodate the boss but not at the expense of feeling powerless.

As you learn to identify, plan, and prioritize your goals, be sure you have a clear understanding of what the boss perceives as system or organization goals. Try to avoid misunderstandings and conflicts by reviewing your vision, mission, and goals with the boss. This allows for an open exchange and dialogue on how you plan to implement your leadership agenda. The boss is less likely to make requests and demands of you that conflict with your agenda or are not in support of it. However, you must stand ready to accept new challenges or tasks that may be asked of you but in which you may not feel confident, competent, or trained.

Accept graciously, reorganize your to-do list, and obtain the necessary knowledge, skills, and training needed to get the job done.

Keeping Track

The following strategies will help you stay the course and improve the quality of your life:

1. Continually assess and reassess your goals and priorities. Monitor your progress and the changes you make along the way. Be sure to remain focused and true to your values.
2. Be open and keep things in perspective. Maintain honesty and evaluate your chosen goals and accomplishments. Do not lose sight of your short-term objectives as you push forward. Take one goal at a time. Watch for short-term gratification and instant success.
3. Stay alert. Observe what is going on around you. Notice your feelings, behaviors, and reactions to life events. Be sensitive to your intuition; listen and act accordingly. It may be reminding you of what is really important. Do not forget your priorities.

4. Become empowered. Advocate for yourself. Learn to express yourself clearly and with confidence. It is important to call attention to your goals and seek guidance when needed. Let others know how they can help you.
5. Take good care of yourself. No one but you can determine what is most important in your life. As you progress in your career, validate yourself by nurturing your professional development: go to school for an advanced degree, attend professional conferences and conventions, join a professional association, and build networks and professional relationships. All of these activities will enrich your life as you seek to fulfill your goals.

Evaluating Progress

As you build strategies and skills in time management, it is important that you monitor your progress. Periodic review and evaluation can help you keep in touch with your own leadership development and focused on prioritizing and accomplishing your important goals. Consider the following questions every four to six months:

- Does my personal mission statement reflect my vision and values?
- Do my goals represent the best of what I am capable of achieving?
- Are my goals focused and centered? Are they broken into the smallest size possible?
- Do I feel fulfilled, challenged, and motivated by these goals?
- Do I have the skills necessary to accomplish these goals?
- What do I need to do to remain inspired and self-disciplined?
- Do I feel empowered to schedule my priorities rather than prioritize what is on my schedule?
- Can I distinguish between what is urgent and what is important?
- Do I maintain an appropriate balance among the various aspects of my life: work, school, family, friends, and community?
- Do I feel in control of my personal and professional life?

Summary

Time is a precious resource. Nurse leaders must learn to conserve their energy and control their time. If you do not compose yourself, your actions and responses will be illogical and shortsighted. Changing your behavior requires you to learn new behavior. You must learn to control your time and use it wisely. Remember that the key to changing your behavior is having a goal or vision. Only with an overall goal and as many subgoals as realistically feasible will you learn to plan and prioritize your time effectively.

Find ways to measure your progress in terms of the chosen goals. Keep track and focused on what you are doing, and make finer and finer adjustments as you are faced with the challenges of each activity. Make sure you have the necessary skills to do the activity. If you do not seek out assistance.

Calm the mind and soul. Balance and prioritize your goals and demands. Do not let time become your master.

REFERENCES

Covey, S. (1989). *The seven habits of highly effective people*. New York: Simon & Schuster.

Lakein, A. (1973). *How to get control of your time and your life*. New York: New American Library.

Mackenzie, R. A. (1972). *The time trap: How to get more done in less time*. New York: McGraw-Hill.

Oncken, W., and Wass, D. (1990). Management time: Who's got the monkey. *Journal of Nursing Administration, 20*(12), 6–9.

Singer, J. (1970). The unholy Bible; a psychological interpretation of William Blake. New York: Putnam.

Ulrich, B. (1985). Time management for the nurse executive. *Nursing Economics, 3*, 318–323.

CHAPTER 11

Performance Measurement

The servant as leader always empathizes, always accepts the person but sometimes refuses to accept some of the person's effort or performance as good enough.

ROBERT K. GREENLEAF (1991)

Performance management is a process designed to allow nurse leaders and team members to work collaboratively on goal setting, giving feedback, reviewing results, and receiving recognition for a job well done. Goals must reflect joint agreement and ownership. The nurse leader must strive to have team members accept and work toward achieving their identified goals. This places the responsibility for performance on the team member.

ROLE RESPONSIBILITIES

Nurse leader
- **Sets specific, numerical expectations as they relate to quality and patient safety and ensures these goals are measurable, achievable, and reasonable. These goals must support patient care needs and provide a sense of accomplishment.**
- **Encourages a balance between the complexity of performance measures and the standards of care. Here the nurse leader must remain firm. Every team member must be encouraged to have measurable targets and take personal responsibility for achieving them.**
- **Participates with team members to examine the goals, action plan, and deadlines against all alternatives.**
- **Reviews and revises system supports and resources necessary to obtain the desired goals.**

- **Follows the progress of the work.** Encourages and reinforces achievement and assists in problem solving as needed.
- **Ensures deadlines and targets are met or modified as needed.**

Team member
- **Helps identify and establish performance goals and standards.** By setting goals, team members accept the responsibility to achieve the results.
- **Develops specific methods for measuring the results and checkpoints for monitoring progress.**
- **Defines the action plan required to accomplish the goals and standards.**
- **Specifies the resources required for the leader, organization, and others to achieve the goals and standards.**
- **Creates the necessary data or documentation to demonstrate the outcomes of goals.**
- **Seeks the necessary support and guidance to revise and renew goals.**

Understanding the roles and responsibilities for performance measurement helps you to guide and motivate your team members to accept the goals and work toward achieving them. It is up to you to let your team members know what you expect. If you fail to communicate your vision, values, and goals clearly, your team members will never know it or do it.

MOTIVATION AND PERFORMANCE

Can you motivate your team members to achieve the outcomes and results of their goals? Do you have what it takes to keep their energy and enthusiasm flowing? Consider the following list of abilities to measure your capacity to motivate team members:

- Give certainty and purposes to others who may have difficulty in achieving the goal themselves.
- Initiate, provide ideas and structure, and balance the risk of failure with the chance of success.
- Provide the financial and human resources to get the job done.
- Strive to foster a positive and caring work environment.
- Create unique ways and opportunities to recognize and reward good work.

- Allow and listen to complaints, opposition, and ideas objectively.
- Willingly delegate and encourage participation in decision making.
- Understand the importance of trust and build loyalty within the team and organization.
- Nurture, support, and encourage shared values of hope, enthusiasm, and compassion for self and others.
- Openly share knowledge, expertise, and experience with team members.
- Provide feedback, using anecdotal notes as a motivational device.
- Acknowledge good performance freely and openly; counsel poor performance in private.
- Ensure that each member of the team is valued and contributes fully.

Nurse leaders have an obligation to assess and determine the strengths and weaknesses of individual team members. You must learn how to use each member's attributes to achieve the best performance possible. To obtain the best, you must focus on where you want to be and what results you want to achieve. Analyze how the team's attributes will contribute to the results you want to achieve. Organize and plan your goals together with team members. Be sure to analyze barriers and attitudes that block your effectiveness or the team's effectiveness to achieve desired results. Learn ways to cope and overcome the barriers and attitudes that impede goal achievement. Try to make a list of obstacles that keep either you or team members from succeeding. Determine what could be done collectively to eliminate some of those obstacles.

> **TIP**
>
> Performance measurement is more than a periodic evaluation. It means identifying a purpose and challenging with opportunity, providing judicious use of incentives, instilling an astute ordering of priorities, and allocating resources where they count most (Greenleaf, 1991).

Measurement is critical to performance. Measurements can be made in the form of quantity, quality, capacity, or some other dimension, depending on the area being measured. When planning a measurement system, consider the following questions:

1. What is to be done?
2. For whom is it to be done?
3. What is wanted, needed, or expected?

4. Is it measurable, realistic, and achievable?
5. How will it be accomplished?
6. Is the work process capable of delivering what is expected?
7. Are changes required in the process?

As you begin to review and revise your performance measurement system, be sure it reflects what team members are doing in the workplace. A sound measurement system will provide early identification of potential problems and actions required to improve patient satisfaction and team members' competence and skill.

QUESTIONS TO GUIDE PERFORMANCE MEASUREMENT

- How do you know when you or your team members are succeeding?
- Do you or your team members have real measurement data that tell them how they are doing?
- Does the organization encourage the use of data to measure its performance goal?

> **TIP**
> As you begin to examine parameters of performance, do not forget to dust off the desk references and manuals and pull out the job standards and job descriptions used to guide clinical practice. These usually are design measurements that provide clear, direct feedback on the behavior for clinical practice.

PERFORMANCE SYSTEMS

Job Descriptions

Performance systems can help nurse leaders to produce results—improved customer satisfaction, a high-performance work environment, patient objectives, increased productivity—while decreasing cost. To get these desired results in patient care delivery, nurse leaders must create and use job-friendly descriptions. Job descriptions set out the necessary job functions, obligations, and responsibilities. When used appropriately, a job description will:

- Help employees understand their duties.
- Orient new employees to the job.
- Improve work flow.
- Develop job specifications.
- Evaluate job performance.
- Clarify relationships among jobs.
- Identify potential training needs.
- Serve as a basis for planning staffing levels or changing staff responsibilities.
- Assist in the hiring and placement of employees.
- Establish line of promotion within the service or department.
- Establish a rational basis for developing a salary structure.

Principles of Performance Management

For a performance management system to achieve results and be successful, nurse leaders must understand the basic principles of performance management:

1. Know the job description and standards of performance for the person who is being evaluated.
2. Remain as objective as possible. Allow the performance measurement to be a true reflection of the performance.
3. Encourage and allow the person being evaluated to set attainable goals, in both the short and long terms.
4. Provide sufficient time for the person being evaluated to examine the performance measurement and discuss any concerns or problems, or deficiencies in performance.
5. Identify ways to improve or strengthen job performance, job enrichers, or morale enhancers.
6. Draft a mutual contract that allows for and encourages growth and career advancement.

The focus of a performance measurement should always be on outcomes of behavior. Consider asking your team members to come up with specific patient care or professional measures of performance. Measure the few most important behaviors. Then explain that these behaviors can be used to:

- Provide feedback.
- Justify merit increases and other compensation adjustments.
- Identify candidates for promotion.

- Confirm hiring decisions.
- Counsel and terminate.

The Performance Dialogue

Prior to conducting a performance evaluation, the nurse leader must establish a dialogue with the team members who will be evaluated. By initiating this contact, the nurse leader encourages openness and provides some guidance on self-appraisal standards and instructions. The person being evaluated is asked to complete a questionnaire on work-related issues prior to the formal dialogue. This exercise allows the person being evaluated to formalize a mechanism to explore and assess her own performance. It also lends some objectivity to the evaluation process and does not solely rely on the nurse leader's personal feelings.

OPENING THE PERFORMANCE EVALUATION DIALOGUE

1. Do you feel the requirements of your job have changed or evolved in the past year?
2. Describe the nature of the bulk of your work, and comment on your assessment of your work performance.
3. Note any important objectives undertaken in the last year, and comment on your achievement of them.
4. What difficulties, unplanned changes in priorities, complexity of tasks, or other factors did you encounter that had effects on the quantity and quality of your nursing care assignments?
5. Comment on those parts of your job you do best. How do your professional knowledge, skills, experience, behavior, and attitudes apply?
6. How has leadership been helpful to you during this period?
7. How could leadership have been more helpful to you?
8. If change in our leadership relationship is a goal for you, what can we each do to help effect that change?
9. Comment on those parts of your work you believe need improvement. What additional professional knowledge, skills, experience, or changes in behavior and attitudes might be helpful?
10. What goals and objectives do you wish to accomplish in the coming year?
11. What actions, training, or assignments do you think should be taken to help achieve your objectives and meet the requirements of your position next year?

Key Elements of Performance Measurement

Performance measurement focuses on a number of important elements:

- *Quality of work.* Accurate, thorough, timely, effective, presentable, appropriate, feasible? Is it at or above the skill and knowledge levels required? If undue leadership effort is required, seek to refine and improve; quality maintained by reducing work volume; must work be redone; adversely affects the patient or others?
- *Volume of acceptable work.* Meets job standards and patient needs; clearly an asset to the nursing unit; takes on extra assignments and tasks; shows initiative to resolve obstacles to productivity?
- *Knowledge of work.* Policies, procedures, regulations, resources, and current trends relating to position; knowledge of changes; practical application to daily duties?
- *Work judgments.* Sound, consistent, reliable; positive effect on self, others; teamwork; promotes workplace harmony; delivers compassionate, appropriate nursing care?
- *Planning and organization.* Plans the sequence of steps; allowances made for foreseeable circumstances; work prioritized effectively to manage demands and achieve goals?
- *Meeting deadlines.* Noncompliance or achievement?
- *Accepts responsibility.* Readily and consistently accepts responsibility; errors admitted and responsibility accepted; effective action taken willingly and swiftly?
- *Accepts direction.* Carried out to the best of ability?
- *Accepts change.* Flexible; adapts satisfactorily to new equipment, procedures, team members?
- *Effective under stress.* Meets regular demands of position; emergency or peak demand periods; unforeseen contingencies?
- *Work coordination.* Good communication and follow-up skills; maintains a smooth flow of work; all appropriate channels used to effect results?
- *Initiative.* Originates projects; produces more efficient methods and procedures?
- *Public contacts.* Courteous and discreet; consistently positive demeanor to public; reflects credit on nursing unit and service and promotes a positive public image?
- *Patient contacts.* Helpful or detrimental; manner professional, sensitive, helpful, firm when necessary; patients handled compassionately and caringly?

- *Employee contacts.* General constructive force; makes positive observations and transmits those of others; seeks mute criticism and fosters relationships; generally cordial and cooperative; avoids becoming inappropriate advocate for others; avoids taking sides in others' work group conflicts; positive influence on others' morale?
- *Compliance with policies and procedures.* Safety, attendance, punctuality, other; noncompliance harmful to nursing unit or service or to work or morale of team members and others who may be affected?

CREATING A SUPPORT SYSTEM

Performance measurement should not be an annual event or occurrence whereby nurse leaders reward or punish team members. Ideally, the performance measurement process should be viewed as ongoing, with the nurse leader and team members equally participating. This shared participation should strengthen the work relationship and relieve the subjective and impressionistic feelings that performance evaluations often give.

To encourage a continuing process of performance evaluation and feedback rather than a yearly event, the nurse leader can initiate a support system with the following key components:

1. Nurse leader support
2. Team support
3. Nurse leader–team member support

Nurse Leader Support

Conducting and accomplishing performance evaluations without prior experience or know-how can be an overwhelming task that leaves nurse leaders feeling guilty or inadequate over their ability to assess performance sufficiently.

To overcome these feeling of inadequacy, nurse leaders can initiate a support system whereby a group of them meet to discuss their problems and identify their feelings about the performance measurement process in general.

When contemplating a focus group on performance evaluation, be sure to consider the following issues:

1. Identify nurse leaders who are interested in discussing their thoughts about performance measurement.
2 Establish a date, time, and place to share ideas on specific issues and problems relating to performance measurement.

3. Seek out potential additional assistance and support from the human resources department.
4. Role-play performance interviews.
5. Conduct peer performance evaluations to become comfortable with the process.
6. If necessary, schedule a follow-up meeting to review the performance process: identify problems, emerging issues, lessons learned, and skills required in the future.

Team Support

An alternative to the traditional individual team member performance evaluation system is the evaluation of a team's accomplishment. The nurse leader can be pivotal in guiding a team to develop criteria by which they can evaluate their performance and productivity. If the nurse leader believes that the team is mature in job duties and functions, then self-evaluation can be an empowering experience.

An evaluation of a team's performance provides information on how well the team collectively works on achieving its goals. The performance process when conducted by the team would include comments by the nurse leader on overall group effectiveness and other measures deemed appropriate. The results would be filed into each team member's personnel folder.

Nurse Leader–Team Support

A nurse leader who has effectively developed teams, facilitated their work, and increased their performance may be ready to have team members evaluate her performance. This evaluation requires team members to establish meaningful criteria that truly reflect the leader's scope of responsibility.

Allowing team members the opportunity to engage in the performance process of their leader suggests that there is a trusting relationship between the leader and her team. The team's honest assessment of the leader can be a constructive experience. It allows the performance measurement process to become an equally valued process by both parties. The nurse leader and team gain a renewed understanding of performance measurement as a way to grow and improve.

FEEDBACK

The use of anecdotal notes is not new to nurses. In the past, nurse leaders have used these notes for clinical performance evaluations. The purpose of the **anecdotal note** was to record the behaviors of those being appraised or evaluated. These notes could be saved and used later when a more formal evaluation process was warranted.

> **TIP**
>
> The process of documenting observations and incidents at the time of the occurrence helps nurse leaders to perform three important functions of the performance measurement process: (1) provide feedback, (2) coach, and (3) make promotion decisions.

Nurse leaders can put feedback, counseling, and coaching into their daily schedule and make anecdotal notes. Start with becoming more observant of those around you. Be present and available to lend a hand at a moment's notice. Do not wait for an accident to happen. If you observe a personal problem or a performance or attitude problem of a team member, be ready to counsel. **Counseling** is a supportive process to help team members define and work through personal problems that might affect their job performance. If, on the other hand, you observe a lack of knowledge about job responsibilities, be ready to coach. Coaching is guiding a team member to the responsibilities of the workplace and helping to remove obstacles to work performance.

When you observe positive actions and behavior by team members, be sure to give appropriate praise and recognition. Then quickly write down what you saw and heard. Describe in a paragraph what the team member did in what setting, under what circumstance, about what issue or problem. Then share this recorded information in a timely manner with the team member. This information can be saved and placed in the team member's personnel folder. Date each anecdotal note at the time it is written and when it was discussed with the team member.

At the time a scheduled performance evaluation is due, the nurse leader will have secured and documented observations of team members that accurately reflect summary feedback and evaluation comments on their performance. This record of documented anecdotal notes removes the surprise of what will emerge during a performance review. Because this information has been recorded on notes and accounted for in earlier discussions between the nurse leader and team member, it cannot be denied at the review. In addition, the nurse leader does not have to recall the past year's performance to formulate judgments for the review. Each anecdotal note is a record in and of itself. If notes are kept correctly, accurately, and regularly, there will be an accumulation of data compiled in each team member's personnel folder to be used whenever a performance review or discussion is warranted.

When a nurse leader provides feedback in a timely fashion, team members are in a position to adapt their behavior more readily. When there is prompt and continuous coaching, team members learn how they are doing and will be able to correct small performance or behavioral issues before they develop into larger ones. Here, team members can track for themselves the areas of work performance that require special attention, improvement, or acknowledgment for a job well done. The key to successful coaching is to recognize when and which behavior is being evaluated.

As you begin to incorporate feedback, counseling, and coaching into your daily routine and skills of leadership, the punitive and negative feelings of performance review dissipate. As the concept and practice of performance measurement become clearer, team members will understand that evaluation is not a one-time event.

TIP

Ongoing feedback, counseling, and coaching help team members gain a sense of professional security, worth, and direction. When the feedback is direct, honest, and sincere, each team member benefits, and the groundwork is created for a successful performance process.

BENEFITS OF CONTINUOUS FEEDBACK

- **Increased motivation and commitment.**
- **Increased team cohesiveness and spirit.**
- **Increased risk-taking behaviors, since team members feel secure and free to be creative.**
- **Increased quality of work and greater commitment to excellence.**
- **Stronger relationships and deeper trust.**
- **Greater inspiration and optimism.**
- **Strengthened self-confidence.**

Nurse leaders who commit to a system of continuous feedback and the use of anecdotal notes are in a better position to assess team members accurately for promotion opportunities. With the accumulation of performance data over time, nurse leaders create a profile that reflects career growth and promotion potential and allows a judgment as to whether the time is right for a job promotion. By accurately reviewing all the performance data—job successes and failures—the nurse leader and team members can judge for themselves their promotion readiness.

Nurse leaders who continuously contribute to team members' personnel records through anecdotal recordings increase the chances of those team members who are truly ready for a job promotion. With complete and updated information available in a team member's folder, the nurse leader can execute promotion decisions fairly.

A long-term benefit of an accurate performance process is the creation of a personnel history with a complete picture of past performances and future aspirations. As a team member builds a career within the organization, the nurse leader can use the personnel history as a guide for promotion, transfer, and financial compensation (merit raise or bonus).

> **TIP**
>
> With consistent record keeping, nurse leaders gain confidence and ease in communicating performance standards and guidelines.

The key to a successful performance measurement is whether it helps team members to recognize behavior that is acceptable as well as that which is unacceptable or needs improvement. This is an excellent way to ensure that the nurse leader is measuring quality according to the Joint Commission on Accreditation of Hospitals (JCAHO) and standard quality indicators (Lathrop, 1995).

When you are ready, assess the unacceptable performance and design a plan that integrates the functions, processes, and dimensions of performance, quality indicators, and quality controls for the year. Assign a block of time to discuss these with the member. When team members' performance is not meeting quality measures, then allocate time to address the severity of the problem and/or performance.

Take the items surrounding the unacceptable performance and lead the team member through the following steps:

1. Establish a mutual understanding and description of the unacceptable performance.

2. Estimate a time frame for each item surrounding the performance by asking the team member how much time she or he will need to address the item.
3. Prioritize the list of items using a ranking technique to make sure the items most critical to the unacceptable performance are handled first.
4. Place an asterisk beside items that will not be covered in the discussion due to time constraints.

This process provides a means for creating an organized agenda that is focused on unacceptable performance and deals with it in a timely, productive fashion. Ghorpade and Chen (1995) suggest that a performance appraisal system driven by quality will improve employee performance, bring about modifications by involving all who are affected, including customers, and place the primary focus on improving behavior.

Successful Performance and Rewards

When team members successfully produce the desired outcomes or achieve the goals, reward them, using as many different rewards as you can think of, formal and informal. Consider the following questions as you explore developing a reward program for your team:

1. How does my organization currently reward successful performance?
2. What rewards can I use to acknowledge successful performance?
3. What kind of formal rewards are available within the organization?
4. What kind of informal rewards are available within the organization?
5. Can I modify or individualize the formal or informal rewards? If so, how?

The message to communicate about rewarding successful performance is that the right behavior really matters. It is important that team members understand that rewards are linked to performance.

> **TIP**
>
> As a nurse leader, you must devise a reward system that demonstrates that good work counts and gets acknowledged.

POTENTIAL REWARDS AND RECOGNITIONS

- **Individual or group incentives (breakfast, lunch, or dinner given by the nurse leader).**
- **Picture of a team member is place on the unit or service where the outstanding performance was accomplished.**
- **Promotion.**
- **Preferred vacation and/or holiday schedule. (Watch out for seniority.)**
- **Preferred lunch or dinner break.**
- **Preferred work assignment.**
- **Yearly subscription to a professional journal.**
- **Paid attendance at a professional development conference or convention.**
- **Letter of recognition.**
- **Box of candy, cookies, or other pleasing sweet.**
- **Tickets for two (to a local movie theater, professional sporting event, concert, etc.).**
- **Gift certificates.**
- **Flowers.**
- **Employee of the Month (or Year) reward.**
- **Ask your team members what they would really want.**

By using a reward system along with continuous feedback via anecdotal notes, you encourage team members to do their best. Fairhurst and Wendt (1993) propose that an effective team-based philosophy serves to secure quality and performance. Use your performance measurement system to specify your expectations and determine what will be measured and how it will be used to reward team members.

SUMMARY

Performance is reality. Nurse leaders must create a clear picture of what is desired, demonstrate and model what is to be done, and then encourage team members to accomplish it.

Be vigilant and prepared to spend the necessary time to translate your vision into reality. You must define the parameters of performance measurement in your own terms and reward accordingly. Stand ready to handle poor performance and behavior, despite explicit directions and expectations. There will always be barriers and obstacles. Anticipate and be prepared to deal with them one at a time.

Learn to let others take responsibility for their goals and action plans. As a coach and facilitator, your responsibility is only to monitor and follow up. Avoid having all the answers, and give team members the opportunity to solve their own problems. This is the best remedy for measuring performance. Allow the performance dial to grow from the inside out. Once team members fully understand their job, give them the encouragement and the resources to obtain success.

REFERENCES

Fairhurst, G., and Wendt, R. (1993). The gap in total quality. *Management Communication Quarterly,* 6(4), 441–451.

Ghorpade, J., and Chen, M. (1995). Creating quality-driven performance appraisal systems. *Academy of Management Executive,* 9(1), 32–39.

Greenleaf, R. K. (1991). *Servant leadership.* New York: Paulist Press.

Lathrop, C. (1995). Coordinating functional chapters for the Joint Commission and performance for departments and teams. *Journal of Healthcare Quality,* 17(1), 14–18.

CHAPTER 12

Computer Technology and Nursing Leadership

DONNA M. COSTELLO-NICKITAS AND MARTIN DORNBAUM

> In a world that is constantly changing, there is no one subject or set of subjects that serve you for the foreseeable future, let alone the rest of your life. The most important skill to acquire now is learning how to learn.
>
> JOHN NAISBITT AND PATRICIA ABURDENE (1985)

Nursing leaders increasingly are using computers and information systems. Information technology in the workplace provides the necessary tools to support health care delivery by offering access to accurate, timely, and relevant information and assisting in data gathering, patient assessments, documentation (charting), monitoring, hospital and home care management plans, and other patient statistics (Hannah, Ball, and Edwards, 1994). Information technology offers nurse leaders greater control over daily operations with the tools to facilitate everyday tasks.

How to Implement Information Technology

1. Recognize and clearly communicate a vision of user-friendly, full-service automation.
2. Develop a structured approach to implementing information technology in the workplace.
3. Make a real commitment to empowering teams to use microcomputers as an aid to patient care and resources management. This requires guidance, formal training, and direct involvement in planning the information systems necessary to manage resources that support organization goals.

4. Find the financial support to create a think tank composed of highly skilled and motivated computer users, regardless of their titled position. This team must address the problems, concerns, and issues related to computer usage. Their purpose is to help disseminate information and the skills required by the new technology.
5. Establish a users' group to share and build on the common experience of using computers for patient care and resources management. This group can help foster shared values and set future activities for microcomputer technology.

> **TIP**
> Success almost always depends on having the right information.

Nursing Applications

The application of technological tools not only enhances the quality of nursing care but keeps leadership capabilities on the cutting edge. For years nurses have relied on computer application software to manipulate words, numbers, data, and designs into support systems for daily workplace functions. (Appendix C contains a list of sources for software.) Computers provide educational applications for teaching, testing, and evaluating nursing staff competencies (Arnold and Pearson, 1992). They can be used to search the periodical literature, conduct research, and process data. With the use of computer-assisted instruction (CAI), interactive video disc (IVD), and new multimedia programs, nurse leaders can support patient and staff educational programming (Bolwell, 1993).

Nurse leaders have relied on CAI programs as a means to individualize instruction in teaching specific skills. These programs engage and stimulate users by providing feedback on program activities. There are programs available on fundamental nursing skills, nursing leadership and management skills, physical assessment skills, monitoring and interpretation skills, critical care nursing skills, and many others. CAIs may consist of drill and practice, tutorials, inquiry and discovery, dialogue, games, or simulations.

A more recent development in computerized education is IVD instruction. These programs combine interactivity with audio and real-time video clips stored optically on a laser disc. Many programs are available in such areas as basic science, health and medicine, and nursing skills, including ethics and legal aspects of nursing, managing the experience of labor and delivery, medication administration and intravenous therapy, physical assessment, monitoring and interpretation, and care of cancer patients.

Another computer tool nurse leaders have come to rely on is CD-ROM databases. These databases offer fast, low-cost access to much of the world's accumulated nursing and medical knowledge. Many programs provide fast and convenient search functions. CD-ROM database titles include numerous unabridged medical textbooks, medical references, journals, abstracts, and directories. Other CD-ROM databases include impressive medical graphics libraries depicting complete human anatomy, medical instruments, and equipment. Nurse leaders can make valuable use of these high-quality-image libraries by incorporating them into proposals, scientific papers, and patient records or by producing overhead projections and 35-mm slides for presentations.

Multimedia CD-ROM is a new form of computerized education that incorporates film and video clips, animations, three-dimensional models, full color plates, and music and spoken narration to illuminate techniques in an interactive format. The user controls the pace and sequence of the program through a mouse or keyboard. Multimedia CD-ROM programs are available on the structure of the human body, the process of conception and birth, medical administration, nutrition, anatomy and physiology, and many others.

By using computer technologies to direct and support nursing and clinical nursing practice, nurse leaders gain the necessary information to define, standardize, and unify nursing practice. The use of these technologies in daily practice enables nurse leaders to make more efficient use of time and information.

> **TIP**
>
> Nursing leaders have turned to computers and information systems to benefit their patients by improving the health care they receive.

COMPUTER APPLICATIONS

Key leadership areas have been affected by the use of computer technologies:

- Patient care services
- Human resources management
- Fiscal resources management
- Education, training, and research
- Staffing and scheduling

Nurse leaders are using a variety of information systems. A review of some of them follows. These systems and other technological tools are cost-effective measures that provide good delivery options for nurse leaders and team members.

Nursing Information Systems

Nursing information systems (NIS) contain nursing and health data that collect, store, process, retrieve, and communicate. NIS are developed in order to deliver nursing services, standardize patient care, and bridge education and research to the practice of nursing (Saba and McCormick, 1986). Nursing information systems are divided into systems that contain the following functions:

- Patient classification or acuity
- Care planning and documentation
- Quality improvement
- Inventory
- Discharge planning
- Performance measurement
- Point-of-care systems

Hospital Information Systems

Hospital information systems (HIS) include information from all clinical and administrative services:

- Patient accounting
- Financial management
- Patient care
- Pharmacy
- Radiology
- Laboratory

Decision Support Systems

Decision support systems (DSS) are vehicles that allow leaders to make informed operating and management decisions based on forecast and "what-if" scenarios (Brown, 1991). These support system programs include:

- Cost accounting
- Case mix
- Departmental and organizational budgeting and forecasting
- Marketing planning

Executive Information Systems

For executive information on the status and performance of the organization, **Executive information systems** (EIS) allow leaders to explore and examine key indicators of organizational performance: cash balance, net income, capital expenditures, patient acuity, census, staffing levels, and the level of patient or physician dissatisfaction or complaints (Simpson, 1992). The executive information system has the capacity to consolidate, interpret, and forecast data, all important for decision making.

BENEFITS OF INFORMATION SYSTEMS

- **Cost-effective and reliable delivery options.**
- **Overall lower educational and training costs because of the one-time purchase fee for each program or package. There are no additional costs for large numbers of staff requiring frequent training.**
- **Little down time.**
- **Easily accessible and available.**
- **No travel and accommodation costs.**
- **Ease of scheduling education, training, and computer usage on an individual basis.**
- **Educational information and content remains consistent throughout each training encounter.**
- **Practice skills are conducted within a safe and secure environment.**
- **Records and training performance are available in hard copy and file disks.**
- **Incorporates a variety of media to address different learning styles.**

Information systems can support nursing practice, research, administration, and education. They are an easy way to manage, document, and monitor patient care as well as administer nursing services and resources within the health care delivery system. They decrease the time between collecting information and making it available to nurse leaders (Romano, 1990), thereby improving organizational problem solving, institutional planning, budgetary patterns, and needs projections.

TIP

Nurse leaders need to have a high degree of information literacy to communicate with their peers.

NURSES ON THE INTERNET

Nurse leaders need to be able to communicate with one another and share information. Now that advanced computer technology and information systems are at our fingertips, nurse leaders have an obligation to get plugged in.

Most nurse leaders realize that to ignore the information superhighway could be detrimental to their career. Those who do not know how to tap into on-line services may lose network opportunities as well as potential revenue-generating opportunities. For each day you do not log onto the Internet or one of the other on-line services, you risk the chance of falling further behind the information elite. When you do log on regularly, you gain the following advantages:

- Become comfortable with the new and emerging vocabulary.
- Understand the new rules for receiving information on demand.
- Become more informed than peers who are not on-line.
- Have greater control over your business.
- Have a research base at your fingertips.

Traveling the Internet

Nurse leaders can become isolated and frustrated by the daily pressures of organizational life. The ability to communicate globally, and debate and discuss issues relevant to nursing education, practice, and research is essential to professional well-being. The Internet connects colleagues all over the world and allows users to find and retrieve information within minutes from a variety of global sources. The Internet is the answer to a network that advances professional and leadership development.

Learning the Language

To travel the information highway, you need a basic understanding of the important terms:

> *Address.* A unique location name that identifies the person sending information. Typically, the first part of the address identifies the user, and the second part of the address gives the user's location—for example: jdoe@delphi.com. The @ symbol separates the user's name from location. An address can also be that of a computer needed for file transfer protocol.

E-mail. The exchange of information over the Internet at its simplest. An e-mail message is an electronic letter from you to another user or to a group of other users.

FAQ (frequently asked questions). A document of helpful information that describes procedures, such as how to post (send) messages to the group, how to stop receiving mail, and how to resolve any problems encountered.

Mailing lists, list servers, and newsgroups. Groups that receive information on a specific topic on a regular basis. The groups are moderated by someone who is knowledgeable on the topic and can facilitate a discussion. The discussion occurs in the form of e-mail sent by the user at the group's address; the e-mail is then posted for all participants to read. The discussion topics may include such subjects as education, research, practice, or contemporary nursing problems and issues.

FTP (file transfer protocol). Similar to obtaining information from a local library. You locate the address of the library and the organization's computer address, go to the FTP library, check the directory, select the materials, and return home.

Archie. An indexing service that offers the opportunity to track information about materials at FTP sites around the world. You can use the Archie and track the content of interest from hundreds of libraries.

Telnet. Allows you to go directly to a remote computer and work. FTP will allow you to check your state university for press releases on nursing issues. Telnet searches the university library's card catalog and databases and works as if you were attached to the on-site network.

Gopher. Allows you to see a series of menus and select topics from each, eventually reaching a source of information. The gopher is equivalent to a librarian; it knows what is in the collection and where to find that information. It offers additional library resources and where to find the material.

Hypertext. Offers the opportunity to read and see information as it would appear in an article, but with a lot more information than a printed page would provide.

World Wide Web (WWW). A WWW document provides the requested information and hypertext links to other related information. If you are a browser, you can see the graphics and hear part of the original document.

On-Line Networks for Nursing

The on-line world offers an exciting opportunity for nurse leaders to get the edge for professional growth. Following are brief descriptions of some of the many networks available:

FITNET. An electronic communications system for Fuld Institute of Technology in Nursing Education (Fitne) that serves as a bulletin board for the posting of news and messages, listing of computer software packages, and direct person-to-person e-mail.

NOVALINK. The Nursing Network Forum contains library files, catalogs, and live conferencing.

DELPHI-SERVICE. The nursing network forum. Access for finding a medical job by forwarding your resumé via e-mail. Access to accredited continuing-education courses through the University of Maryland School of Nursing to the message board where you can contribute to many nursing-related discussions.

ANA*NET. The American Nurses Association network database compiled to further the goals of fostering high standards of nursing, stimulating the professional development of nurses, advancing the economic and general welfare of nursing, and working to improve the health standards and services for all people. By using ANA*Net, the user is linked to informational databases. Indexes to journals, articles and newsletters are available, as well as bulletin board and e-mail services.

Databases for Nursing Professionals

There are several database resources in the areas of human and financial management. Following are brief descriptions of some of them:

E.T. Net. An on-line computer conference network links developers and users of interactive technology in health care education.

NUCARE (Nursing CAre REsearch). Provides opportunities to exchange information significant to nursing care research.

Workplace Advocacy Information Database (WAID). Synthesizes information from public electronic libraries and other sources. This database also indicates American Nurses Association (ANA) activities on given topics and ANA governance information.

Nurse Contracts. Contains information for each state nursing association contract and is available only to these associations.

Human Resources Information Network (HRIN). Deals with employment and collective bargaining issues.

Nurse Wages. Contains a number of public sources of nurse's wages, including wages for nursing school faculty, employment settings other than hospitals, and temporary RNs.

Lexis. A full text database of an immense body of case law, administrative materials, and other sources of law-related information.

Nexus. The world's largest database offering full text of news and business publications, medical and financial information, press releases, television scripts, magazines, and more.

RESEARCH PUBLICATIONS AND DATABASES

For current research and clinical practice issues, consult the indexes of CINAHL and Medline. Both are valuable resources to search when planning, implementing, and evaluating research.

CINAHL. The Cumulative Index to Nursing and Allied Health Literature provides access to all nursing journals and other publications.

Grateful Med/Medline. In the National Library of Medicine's database of more than 6 million citations to biomedical articles. Special databases on AIDS, cancer, and other topics are offered.

SUMMARY

A well-designed computer information system can free up valuable time by providing readily accessible data. Information systems can assist nurse leaders by providing a structure, definition, and uniformity to nursing practice within the organization. By providing instant, accurate, and reliable data, nurse leaders can support and facilitate decision making by team members. Smart nurse leaders will engage in computer technology to increase nursing's overall efficiency and professional accountability. This technology will supply the means and potential to improve patient care and eliminate nursing's isolation from the rest of the organization. As the boundaries of nursing broaden and medical techniques become more complex and sophisticated, new roles for "nursing informatic leaders" will develop.

REFERENCES

Arnold, J., and Pearson, G. (1992). *Computer applications in nursing education and practice*. New York: National League for Nursing.

Bolwell, C. (1993). *Directory of educational software for nursing*. New York: National League for Nursing.

Brown, R. (1991, March). The evolution of executive information systems. *Systems 3X/400*, 26–34.

Hannah, K. J., Ball, M. J., and Edwards, M. J. A. (1994). *Introduction to nursing informatics*. New York: Springer-Verlag.

Naisbitt, J., and Aburdene, P. (1985). *Reinventing the corporation*. New York: Warner Books.

Romano, C. A. (1990). Informatics: preparation for new nursing rules. *Nursing and Healthcare: the supplement, 41*, 1–2.

Saba, V. K., and McCormick, K. A. (1986). *Essentials of computers for nursing*. Philadelphia: Lippincott.

Simpson, R. (1992). Why executive information systems are important. *Nursing Management, 23*(2), 8–19.

Appendix A

Worksheet for Designing a Planned Change

Step 1: Identifying the Problem

During this first step, the foundation is laid for solving the problem. The main objective is problem identification; the challenge is to develop a clear statement that adequately describes the problem.

All problem statements should contain two components: the "as-is" condition and the "desired state."

As is Fifteen percent of all staff nurse annual performance reviews are completed late.

Desired state All staff nurse performance reports are completed on time.

The as-is component describes the problem as it exists. In this example, staff nurse performance will be accomplished on time. Not conforming to this standard could be time wasting and have an impact on the morale and motivation of staff nurses.

How to Write As-Is Statements

- Be specific and objective.
- Do not include causal statements.
- Do not offer solutions.
- Do not be overly broad.

How to Write the Desired Statements

- Describe the focus of action.
- Be specific and objective.
- Focus on the forces that will help solve the problem.
- Identify the forces that are barriers to solving the problem.

Moving from As-Is to the Desired State

1. Decide on the problem you want to solve.
2. Informally gather the information about it.
3. Write a problem statement that includes an as-is as well as a desired state.
4. If the problem is not specific enough, return to Step 1 after you have collected data in Step 2.
5. Refine the problem statement.

STEP 2: ANALYZING THE PROBLEM

Define the nature and cause (or causes) of the problem. The important elements in this step are the data or information about the problem. The goal of this step is to uncover the potential causes of the problem. Use bar charts, Pareto charts, cause-and-effect analysis, histograms, and check sheets to collect and analyze the data.

How to Analyze Problems

1. Identify the potential causes of the problem.
2. Collect data about the potential causes.
3. Use data to select the key or root causes of the problem.

STEP 3: GENERATING POTENTIAL SOLUTIONS

Search for as many solutions as possible to shrink the problem. Look at all the possible solutions, including using your imagination, past experiences, and experts or consultants in the field. Generate a list of potential solutions. Be sure to review and clarify the solutions with team members so that there is agreement and understanding. Sometimes solutions can be reduced, combined, or eliminated.

How to Search for Potential Solutions

1. Review the problem statement, data, and all the key cause or causes.
2. List all the possible solutions.
3. Carefully review and clarify the potential solutions with team members so that each member understands the impact of each potential solution.

Step 4: Selecting and Planning the Solution

Selecting the best solution or set of solutions and the plan to implement them takes time, energy, and a system of evaluation. This includes knowing how to evaluate each potential solution against a list of criteria, such as a set of rules, standards, or tests on which a judgment or decision is based.

How to Evaluate a Solution or Set of Solutions

1. *Control.* Is the team in a position to implement the solution?
2. *Effectiveness.* Does the solution solve the problem? Is this solution likely to achieve the desired state?
3. *Patient satisfaction.* Will the solution increase patient satisfaction?
4. *Conformance to requirements.* Will the solution better meet the requirement, resulting in increased patient satisfaction?
5. *Time.* How long will it take to implement the selected solution?
6. *Cost of quality.* Will the solution reduce the cost of nonconformance?
7. *Acceptability.* Will team members accept the solution? Can the team adapt to the change required?

After the solution is selected, a plan is developed for implementing it. For the plan to succeed, it must contain specific tasks, assignments, and timetables. The plan should also contain alternative actions—that is, action to take if the plan is not successful or new opportunities present themselves.

How to Select and Implement a Solution

1. Develop criteria for evaluating each potential solution.
2. Agree on the criteria, and judge each solution.
3. Select the best solution.
4. Develop a plan to implement the solution.
5. Include a strategy for obtaining commitment to the plan from team members.
6. Develop a alternative plan as a back-up should you face challenges or surprises.
7. Develop a way to measure the success or failure of the solution.

Step 5: Implementing the Solution

Once the solution has been fully designed and a blueprint established, begin the implementation. Monitor all progress by using a simple checklist that includes:

- The tasks
- Team member assignments and responsibilities
- Dates and time frame of tasks to be accomplished
- Ways to collect data for evaluation
- Alternative plans to deal with crises or opportunities

How to Implement the Solution

1. Put the solution into action.
2. Monitor all actions.
3. Collect data for evaluation.
4. If necessary, implement alternative plans as developed.

Step 6: Evaluating the Solution

All implemented solutions must be evaluated. There is no other way of measuring the success of the recommended solution or set of solutions. Start by comparing the data collected after the solution is in place with the desired state. Go back to the original problem statement:

As is	Fifteen percent of all staff nurse annual performance reviews are completed late.
Desired state	All staff nurse performance reports are completed on time.
After solution, data showed	No late reports.

Appendix B

Directory of National Nursing Organizations

American Academy of Ambulatory
  Care Nursing
East Holly Ave.
Box 56
Pitman, NJ 08071-0056
Tel. 609-256-2300

American Academy of Nurse
  Practitioners
Capitol Station
LBJ Building
P.O. Box 12846
Austin, TX 78711
Tel. 521-442-4262
Fax 521-442-6469

American Assembly for Men
  in Nursing
P.O. Box 31753
Independence, OH 44131
Tel. 216-524-3504

American Association of Colleges
  of Nursing
One Dupont Circle
Suite 530
Washington, DC 20036
Tel. 202-463-6930
Fax 202-785-8320

American Association of Critical-Care
  Nurses
101 Columbia
Aliso Viejo, CA 92656-1491
Tel. 800-899-2226
Fax 714-362-2020

American Association of Legal Nurse
  Consultants
500 N. Michigan Ave.
Suite 1400
Chicago, IL 60011
Tel. 312-670-0550
Fax 312-661-0769

American Association of Nurse
  Attorneys
720 Light St.
Baltimore, MD 21230
Tel. 410-752-3318
Fax 410-752-8295

American College of Nurse-Midwives
818 Connecticut Ave., NW
Suite 900
Washington, DC 20006
Tel. 202-728-9860
Fax 202-728-9897

APPENDIX B DIRECTORY OF NATIONAL NURSING ORGANIZATIONS 185

American Holistic Nurses'
Association
4101 Lake Boone Trail
Suite 201
Raleigh, NC 27607
Tel. 919-787-5181

American Nurses Association
600 Maryland Ave., SW
Suite 100 West
Washington, DC 20024-2571
Tel. 202-554-4444
Fax 202-554-2262

American Nurses Foundation
600 Maryland Ave., SW
Suite 100 West
Washington, DC 20024
Tel. 202-554-4444
Fax 202-554-2262

American Organization of Nurse
Executives
840 N. Lake Shore Dr.
Chicago, IL 60611
Tel. 312-422-2800
Fax 312-422-4503

American Psychiatric Nurses'
Association
6900 Grove Rd.
Thorofare, NJ 08086
Tel. 609-848-7990

American Society for Long Term Care
Nurses
660 Lonely Cottage Dr.
Upper Black Eddy, PA 18972-9313
Tel. 610-847-5396
Fax 610-847-5063

Association of Child and Adolescent
Psychiatric Nurses, Inc.
1211 Locust St.
Philadelphia, PA 19107
Tel. 800-826-2950
Fax 215-545-8147

Association of Community Health
Nursing
407 North Park Ave.
Indianapolis, IN 46202
Tel. 371-274-2129
Fax 317-274-2996

Association of Nurses in AIDS Care
704 Stonyhill Rd.
Suite 106
Yardley, PA 19067
Tel. 215-321-2371
Fax 215-321-2370

Association of Operating Room
Nurses
2170 S. Parker Rd.
Suite 300
Denver, CO 80231-5711
Tel. 303-755-6300

Association of Pediatric Oncology
Nurses
11512 Allecingie Parkway
Richmond, VA 23235
Tel. 804-379-9150

Association of Rehabilitation Nurses
5700 Old Orchard Rd., 1st Fl.
Skokie, IL 60077-1057
Tel. 708-966-3433

Association of Women's Health, Obstetric, and Neonatal Nurses
700 14th St., NW
Suite 600
Washington, DC 20005
Tel. 202-662-1600
Fax 202-737-0575

Drug and Alcohol Nursing Association, Inc.
660 Lonely Cottage Dr.
Upper Black Eddy, PA 18972-9313
Tel. 610-847-5396
Fax 610-847-5063

Emergency Nurses Association
216 Higgins Rd.
Park Ridge, IL 60068
Tel. 708-698-9400
Fax 708-698-9406

Interagency Council on Library Resources for Nursing
c/o Medical Library
Monmouth Medical Center
300 Second Ave.
Long Branch, NJ 07740
Tel. 908-870-5170

National Association of Directors of Nursing Administration in Long Term Care
10999 Reed Hartman Hwy.
Suite 229
Cincinnati, OH 45242
Tel. 800-222-0539

National Association of Hispanic Nurses
1501 16th St., NW
Washington, DC 20036
Tel. 202-387-2477
Fax 202-797-9353

National Association of Neonatal Nurses
1304 Southpoint Blvd.
Suite 280
Petaluma, CA 94954-6859
Tel. 707-762-5588
Fax 707-762-0401

National Black Nurses Association
1012 10th St., NW
Washington, DC 20001
Tel. 202-393-6870

National Consortium of Chemical Dependency Nurses
1720 Willow Creek Circle
Suite 519
Eugene, OR 97402
Tel. 800-876-2236
Fax 503-485-7372

National Federation for Specialty Nursing Organizations
East Holly Ave.
Box 56
Pitman, NJ 08071-0056
Tel. 609-256-2333
Fax 609-589-7463

National Gerontological Nursing Association
7250 Parkway Drive
Suite 510
Hanover, MD 21076
Tel. 800-723-0560

National League for Nursing
350 Hudson Street
New York, NY 10014
Tel. 212-989-9393

National Nurses in Business Association
1000 Burnett Ave.
Suite 450
Concord, CA 94520
Tel. 510-356-2642
Fax 510-356-2654

North American Nursing Diagnosis Association
1211 Locust St.
Philadelphia, PA 19107
Tel. 215-545-8105
Fax 215-545-8107

Nurses Education Fund, Inc.
555 West 57th Street
New York, NY 10019
Tel. 212-582-8820, ext 806

Nurse Healers–Professional Associates
175 Fifth Ave.
New York, NY 10001
Tel. 212-886-3776

Nurses House, Inc.
350 Hudson Street
New York, NY 10014
Tel. 212-989-9393, ext. 232

Nursing Network on Violence Against Women International
University of Massachusetts, School of Nursing
Amherst, MA 01003
Tel. 413-545-5085

Transcultural Nursing Society
College of Nursing and Health
Madonna University
36600 Schoolcraft Rd.
Livonia, MI 48150
Tel. 313-591-8320

Visiting Nurse Association of America
3801 E. Florida Ave.
Suite 900
Dever, CO 80210
Tel. 303-753-0218
Fax 303-753-0258

Appendix C

Computer Software for Nurse Leaders

Addison-Wesley Nursing
1 Jacob Way
Reading, MA 01867
800-950-5544

Alpha Media
P.O. Box 1719
Maryland Heights, MO
 63043-1719
800-832-1000

American Journal of Nursing
555 West 57th Street
New York, NY 10019
800-223-2282

Argosy Network Corporation
618 Grassmere Park Rd.
Suite 17
Nashville, TN 37211-3643
800-633-8643

Arnett Development Corporation
P.O. Box 6326
North Augusta, SC 29841
803-279-6325

C&D Computer Enterprises, Inc.
P.O. Box 2278
Glen Elly, IL 60138-2278
708-653-3555

Computerized Educational Systems
P.O. Box 536905
Orlando, FL 32853-6905
800-275-1474

Darox Interactive
7825 Fay Ave.
Suite 200
La Jolla, CA 92037
800-733-1010

DataStar
4220 98th Street
Suite 101
Edmonton, Alberta, T6E6A1 Canada
403-463-3327

FITNE
5 Depot St.
Athens, OH 45701
614-592-2511

Appendix C Computer Software for Nurse Leaders

Health Sciences Center for
  Educational Resources
Center Distribution, T-252
Mail Stop SB-56
University of Washington
Seattle, WA 98195
206-685-1156

Health Sciences Consortium
201 Silver Cedar Ct.
Chapel Hill, NC 27514
919-942-8731

J. B. Lippincott Company
Department of Audiovisual Media
227 East Washington Square
Philadelphia, PA 19106-3780
800-523-2945

MSI, Inc.
Diamond Custom Training Software
P.O. Box 6952
Boise, ID 83707-6952
800-359-2996

National League for Nursing
350 Hudson St.
New York, NY 10014
800-669-9656

Open Learning Agency
Marketing Division
4355 Mathisi Race
Burnaby, BC, V5G4S8 Canada
800-663-1653

Professional Development Software
P.O. Box 2063
Chapel Hill, NC 27515
919-932-5013

Williams and Wilkins
Electronic Media Division
428 E. Preston St.
Baltimore, MD 21202
800-527-5597

Glossary

Anecdotal note A record used to document the behaviors of those being appraised or evaluated.
Boss time Time requirements imposed by the boss.
Brainstorming A technique that allows the brain to let go and produce a flood of thoughts and ideas.
Change A deviation from an established pattern. It requires creating a new system.
Change agent An individual who prepares the way for change; a facilitator who enables change to happen; someone whose function serves to identify and repair the breakdowns in the change process.
Collective decision making process A process that—although it is time-consuming—generates total team involvement in finding creative solutions for problem solving.
Collaborative leadership A leadership approach in which team members have a role and a voice in patient care decisions.
Communication A way to be in touch, joined with others, to inform, say, and transfer ideas, feelings, and thoughts.
Communication plan A map that sets out the objectives, implications, training requirements, and progress reports of the planned change.
Compassionate leadership A leadership style characterized by openness, receptivity to ideas, caring, dignity, and respect toward others.
Counseling A supportive process to help team members define and work through personal problems that might affect their job performance.
Direct question A question that leads to a response from a specific group member.
Dysfunctional conflict A disruptive and counter-productive conflict that destroys group process.
Empowerment A process of enhancing feelings of self-efficacy among organization members.
Executive information systems Software systems that contain the status and performance of the organization.

Facilitator A person who has the capacity to help group members grow and develop a psychic bond that promotes unity and a special connectedness that goes beyond the nature of the work.

Feminine values A set of core values that focus on process rather than product, including wholeness, interconnectedness, equality, diversity, and collaboration.

General question A question that leads to a response from any group member.

Head-to-head meeting A session in which individuals representing many functional areas gather into one room to discuss a range of issues and challenges.

Horizontal violence An intergroup conflict among people in the same stratum in the hierarchy.

Hospital information systems Software systems that contain information from all clinical and administrative services.

Index-card meeting Team members write questions or comments on a 3 by 5 inch card, which is routed through the organization to someone who has the knowledge and authority to respond appropriately within 24 hours.

Influence A skill used to gain power in interpersonal situations.

Interviewing A structured technique that is an effective means for collecting information from an individual job applicant.

Interview process The opportunity to determine the potential for a good match between the applicant and the job specifications.

Keeping track A time management plan that will reduce the number of crises in your life and will lead to increased to personal satisfaction, effectiveness, and results.

Leadership More than taking charge, holding a position of rank or authority, or having a title—it is knowing what is right and necessary.

Management time Time that must be devoted to meeting the needs and demands made by team members, peers and colleagues, and the boss.

Mentoring A process of guiding, coaching, and advising someone who is less experienced.

Networking A process of gaining access to crucial information, advice, contacts, and visibility.

Nontraditional leadership A leadership style encompassing a feminine approach of shared power, flexibility, inclusion, and equality.

Nurse leader Positions and prioritizes patient care with the organization's vision and focuses on meeting patients' needs.

Nurse manager Focuses on the bottom line, with goal attainment tied to cost, rules, and regulations over vision and values.

Nursing information systems Software systems that contain nursing and health data.

Partnership A desired relationship between parties seeking to work together toward a common goal.

Peer and colleague time Time requirements made by a peer or colleague for a special request or consultation.

Performance management A process designed to allow nurse leaders and team members to work collaboratively on goal setting, giving feedback, reviewing results, and receiving recognition for a job well done.

Personal best A process that fosters team members to "give it their best shot" when achieving organizational tasks or goals.

Please-arrange-to-see-me meeting A prearranged meeting time for which a few hours of each day is set aside and divided into 15-minute segments to see team members.

Policy A set of principles that govern action toward a given end.

Policy checklist A set of rules to engage in the policy process.

Politics A competition for scarce resources.

Power brokers Principle players of workplace politics and policy.

Problem-solving process A strategy for nurse leaders to use in resolving problems and promoting change.

Relay question A question designed to give those in the group who either know the relevant facts or haven't yet contributed a chance to respond.

Resumé A marketing tool that reflects the candidate's qualifications on paper.

Return question A follow-up question that leads to returning to the group member who asked the initial question.

Self-directed team An interactive group of employees who are responsible for a whole work process or segments that deliver a product or service.

Shared governance model A management philosophy that promotes and supports decentralized power sharing and decision making.

Stand-up meeting A simple and brief meeting of no more than 20 minutes with direct reports designed to provide support and intervention in areas that may present problems.

Sit-down meeting A meeting at the end of the day to analyze daily operations and patient care activities.

Successful leadership A leadership style that is flexible and trusting, builds support, and thrives on chaos and uncertainty.

Team building An ongoing process that involves deliberate attention and planned effort.

Team effectiveness A measure of how well a nursing team creates and maintains excellence in the clinical care of patients.

Time management An ongoing process of clarifying your vision, identifying long-range goals; and organizing a daily, weekly, and monthly calendar.

Traditional leadership A leadership style dominated by the masculine traits of competitiveness, independence, aggressiveness, decisiveness, and self-reliance.

Vision A preferred future, a desirable or ideal state.

Index

80/20 rule, 58

A

Aburdene, Patricia, 17, 170
Accountability, empowerment model and, 45, 53
Acquiring power, 31–32
Action plans, 143
Addresses, 175
Administrative support, 77
Agendas, 19, 100
ANA*NET (American Nurses Association network database), 177
Anecdotal notes, 163–166
Applicants
    linking to organization, 119
    meeting, 121
    questions to avoid, 122
    sample questions for, 120–121
    spotting potential problems, 123
Archie, 176
As-is statements, 180, 181
Attitude, 34
Authority, 50

B

Backer, B. J., 48
Barriers
    to change, 80
    to empowerment, 46
    to team development, 69

Behavior
    and empowerment, 43
    of feminine leaders, 25
    nurse leaders as role models, 52, 125, 127–128
    political, 30
    respectful, 127–128, 130
    supporting caring workplace, 126–128
    of team members, 67
Belasco, James A., 75
Belenky, M. F., 20
Bennis, Warren, 1, 3, 31, 61
Bernay, T., 25
Blake, William, 139
Blame, 103
Block, P., 61
Body language, 126
Bolman, L. G., 3
Boss time, 152
Brainstorming, 49–50, 141
Bureaucracy, 45–46
Burns, J., 14
Byham, W. C., 49

C

Calendars, 145, 145f, 150
Cantor, D. W., 25
Career development, 111–112
Carlson-Catalano, J., 51
Categorizing priorities, 146–147
CD-ROM databases, 172
Champy, J., 4, 6, 22, 42

---

f indicates information that can be found in a figure.

193

Change, 75–90
  creating political, 40
  defined, 76
  evaluating, 84–85
  facilitating, 23, 77, 79–80, 93
  flexibility and, 89
  human aspect of, 82–84
  mapping, 88–89*f*
  need for, 79
  planned, 180–183
  preparing for, 77–78
  principles of, 76
  problem solving and, 85–86, 181
  as process, 75–76
  resistance to, 77, 80, 83, 133
  stating areas to, 180–181
  strategy for, 80–81
Change agents, 76–77, 78, 81
Chen, M., 167
Chin, P. L., 44
CINAHL (Cumulative Index to Nursing and Allied Health Literature), 178
Clinchy, B. M., 20
Coaching
  team members and, 164–165
  teams, 50
Colleagueship
  allowing time for, 151
  building, 50–51
  team building and, 65
Collective decision making, 50–51
Commitment
  fostering, 136–137*f*
  to goals, 143
  teamwork and, 63, 70–71
Communication plan, 81–82
Communications
  building consensus with, 21
  change and, 81–82, 85
  and corporate language, 19–20
  effective, 130–132
  gender-specific styles of, 20
  of goals, 143
  influence and, 34, 37–39, 92
  meetings and, 12–13, 101
  nurse leaders as communicators, 128–131, 134–135
  open-ended questions, 65
  personalized, 82
  promoting, 52, 96
  respectful, 127–128
  summarizing, 132
  supportive workplaces and, 128–132
  teams and, 62, 63, 69, 70
  time management and, 150
  of trust, 82
  verbal and nonverbal, 126, 128–129
  of vision, 11–12
Computer-assisted instruction (CAI), 171
Computers, 170–179
  applications for nurses, 171–173
  benefits of, 174
  CD-ROM databases, 172
  interactive video discs, 171–172
  Internet, 175–177
  on-line databases, 177–178
Conflict
  in groups, 46
  politics and, 29
  resolving, 101–106
Confusion, 77
Consensus, 21, 97–98
Control
  of decision making, 133
  empowerment model and, 44–45
  leadership and, 18
  sharing, 48
Coombs, W., 62
Core values, 2–3, 19–20
Corporate language, understanding, 19–20
Counseling team members, 164
Cover letters, 118–119, 118*f*
Creating teams, 49–50, 59–60
Credibility, 20, 131
Cumulative Index to Nursing and Allied Health Literature (CINAHL), 178

D

Databases
  ANA*NET, 177
  CD-ROM, 172
  for nursing professionals, 177–178
Deal, T. E., 3
Decision making
  by teams, 49
  collective, 50–51
  controlling process of, 133
  earning right for, 37–39
  empowerment and, 44
  understanding rules of, 19, 36
Decision support systems (DSS), 173
Delegating, 148–149

Deliverables, 85
DELPHI-SERVICE, 177
DePress, M., 4
Desired statements, 180, 181
Difficult people, 94–95, 103, 104–105
Diversity, 98
Dornbaum, Martin, 170–179
Dress, 34
Duck, J. D., 86
Dysfunctional conflict, 101–102

E

E.T. Net, 177
Economic basis for change, 79
Effectiveness
 of communications, 128–132, 134–135
 of groups, 91–92
 leadership qualities for, 9–10
 Personal Effectiveness Profile, 64f
 of teams, 57–58
 of women, 25
80/20 rule, 58
E-mail
 change and, 81
 mailing lists and, 176
 on-line networks and, 177
 resumés and, 177
Empathic listening, 11, 127, 132
Employees
 creating personnel histories, 166
 evaluating, 161–162
 feedback for, 164–167
 hiring, 115–123
 job descriptions for, 158–159
 see also Team members
Employment databases, 177, 178
Empowerment, 42–55
 access to information and, 53
 authority and, 50
 communication skills for, 127, 128
 framework for, 54
 model for, 46–49
 power and, 43–44
 promoting, 44–45, 52–53
 of team members, 42–44, 46–47, 127–128
 of teams, 54
Energy clocks, time management and, 146
Energy thermostat, monitoring, 136f
Enthusiasm, 21, 83, 131
Environmental changes, 84

Evaluating change, 84–85
Evaluating time management, 153
Executive information systems (EIS), 174
Expectations
 of feminine leadership, 18
 resolving conflict and, 103
 sharing with staff, 11–12
Expertise, 53
Eye contact, 33–34

F

Facilitation, 93–94
Facilitators
 as change agents, 77
 characteristics of, 91, 92
 dealing with difficult people, 94–95, 105–106
 diversity and, 98
 for group meetings, 101
 meeting dynamics and, 101
 role of, 93–96
Failure, 135
Fairhurst, G., 168
FAQ (frequently asked questions), 176
Feedback
 benefits of, 164, 165–167
 encouraging, 11
 giving, 10
 performance evaluations and, 163–164
 team management and, 71
Feelings, 94–95
Feminine leadership, 15–26
 attracting participation, 20
 behavior of, 25
 feminine values and, 19–20
 goals of, 18, 20–21
 power and, 18f, 21–23
 results from, 21, 24
 spider web model of, 16, 17
 strategies of, 23–24, 26
 style of, 17–18, 18f
 see also Leadership
Feminine values, emphasizing, 19–20
Fierman, J., 111
Finances, 85, 174
FITNET, 177
Flexibility, 87
Focus
 in communications, 132
 during change, 83

Focus (continued)
  group meetings and, 101
  grouping goals for, 143–144
  saving time with, 149–150
  team building and, 65
  time management and, 141
Followers, 6, 8
Frankwick, B., 80
FTP (file transfer protocol), 176
Fuld Institute of Technology in Nursing Education, 177

G

Gender-specific communications, 20
Georges, C. A., 48
Ghorpade, J., 167
Gibson, C. H., 44
Gilligan, C., 17
Goals
  acting on, 143
  balancing with interpersonal relationships, 21
  change and, 80
  designing statements of, 180, 181
  of feminine leadership, 18, 20–21
  formulating, 142–143, 142*f*
  grouping, 143–144
  identifying, 11
  as influence on groups, 92
  for meetings, 99
  notebooks for, 144*f*
  and personal mission statements, 141, 142*f*, 153
  rewards for achieving, 143
  teamwork and, 62
  tracking achievement of, 152–153
  vision and, 62
Goldberg, N. R., 20
Gopher, 176
Gouillart, F. J., 109–110
Grateful Med/Medline, 178
Greenleaf, Robert K., 107, 155, 157
Grief, 77
Group meetings, 99–101
Grouping goals, 143–144
Groups, 91–106
  chemistry of, 100
  conflict in, 46
  facilitating, 95–96
  managing, 97–98
  measuring effectiveness of, 91–92
  meetings, 99–101
  members influence on, 92
  variables in, 92–93

H

Hand shakes, 33–34
Head-to-head meetings, 10–11
Health care industry
  patriarchal values of, 15
  transforming, 28
  women in, 22, 23
Health care organizations, empowerment model and, 44–45
Heim, P., 26
Helgesen, S., 16, 22, 26
Hidden agendas, 19
High-peak activities, 147
Hiring employees, 115–123, 158–159
Holladay, S., 62
Honesty, 8
Horizontal violence, 46
Hospital information systems (HIS), 173
Human needs, 82–84
Human Resources Information Network (HRIN), 178
Human resources management, 107–124
  hiring employees, 115–123
  job descriptions, 158–160
  market-focused leadership, 109–110
  matching people to functions, 111
  mentoring, 112–113
  networking, 113–114
Hutt, M., 80
Hypertext, 176

I

Index-card meetings, 13
Influence
  gaining, 32–34
  meetings and, 81
  on policy, 37–38
Information
  empowerment and, 53
  financial, 174
Information systems
  benefits of, 174
  implementing, 170–171

types of, 173–174
Inspiration, 5
Interactive video discs (IVD), 171–172
Internet, 175–177
Interpersonal changes, 85
Interpersonal relationships, 21
Interpersonal skills, 7, 93, 108
Interruptions, 150
Interviewing applicants, 119–123
   guidelines for interviews, 120
   linking applicant to organization, 119f
   preparing for, 121
   questions to avoid, 122
   sample questions for, 120–121
   spotting potential problems, 123

J

Jacob, R., 55
Jeffries, E., 53, 61, 63, 91
Job descriptions, 158–160
Joint Commission on Accreditation of Hospitals (JCAHO), 166

K

Kanter, R. M., 53, 76
Katzenback, J., 65
Keeping-track process, 139
Koerner, J. E., 114
Kouzes, J., 5, 126

L

Lakein, A., 146
Leaders
   characteristics of, 126
   encouraging others, 6, 7
   establishing vision, 4, 5
   feminine, 25
   and followers, 6, 8
   fostering teams, 60
   for group meetings, 100
   interpersonal skills of, 7
   managing conflict, 102, 105–106
   mentoring of, 112–113
   problem solving and, 3
   qualities of, 1, 3, 4f, 9–10
   roles of, 9–10
   self-knowledge skills for, 2–3
   as servant, 155
   stress and, 63–64
   team, 62, 66–68
   team success and, 58
   versus managers, 3–6, 4f
   see also Nurse leaders
Leadership
   collaborative, 42–43
   contributions to workplace, 125–128
   as control, 18
   evaluating, 160
   feminine, 15–26, 18f
   management and, 1–14
   market-focused, 109–110
   masculine traits in, 15
   nontraditional, 16
   politics and, 30–31
   principle-centered, 2
   qualities of effective, 9–10
   reshaping, 25
   shared governance model, 46
   skills and, 7, 8
   trust and, 2
   see also Feminine leadership
Leading groups, 91–106
Learning, 52
Legal databases, 178
Lewis-Ford, B., 103
Lexis, 178
List servers, 176
Listening, empathic, 11, 127, 132
Lorifice, Mary Ellen, 125–138
Loss, 77
Low-peak activities, 147

M

Mailing lists, 176
Management
   decision support systems and, 173
   leadership and, 1–14
   self, 8
   setting time for, 151
   of teams, 62, 71–72
   see also Human resources management; Performance management; Time management

Managers
  qualities of, 4f, 5
  versus leaders, 3–6, 4f
Managing teams, 62, 71–72
Market-focused leadership, 109–110
Marketing philosophy, 110
Mason, D. J., 48
Measurement, *see* Performance measurement
Medline, 178
Meetings, 10–11
  agendas for group, 100
  dynamics of, 101
  group, 99–101
  resolving conflict and, 103
  time management and, 150, 151–152
  types of, 10–13, 81
Menke, K., 29
Mentoring, of team members, 112–113
Michael, D., 36
Mind-set, shifting, 84
Mission statements
  formulating personal, 141, 142f, 153
  role of leaders and, 53
  teamwork and, 62
Mistakes, 131
Mock staffing, 132
Montisano-Marchi, N., 50
Morale, 6
Motivation
  factors in workplace, 70, 71f
  performance and, 156–158
  reasons for, 54
  teams and, 63
Murrell, K., 54

N

Naisbitt, John, 17, 170
Nanus, Burt, 1, 3, 31, 61
National Library of Medicine database, 178
Negotiation, 18f, 32–33
Networking
  building a support base, 30–31
  building colleagueship, 50–51
  guidelines for, 113–114
  on the Internet, 175, 177
  policy initiatives and, 39–40
Newsgroups, 176
Newsletters, 81
Nexus, 178

Nonverbal communications, 126, 128–129, 131
Notebooks, for goals, 144f
NOVALINK, 177
NUCARE (Nursing Care Research), 177
Nurse Contracts, 178
Nurse leaders
  becoming political, 29–30
  behaviors supporting workplace, 126–128
  as career guides, 111–112
  as change agents, 23, 45–46, 75–77, 79–80, 87
  change and, 82–86
  collaborative leadership and, 42–43
  computers and, 170–179
  dealing with difficult people, 94–95, 104–105
  delegating, 148–149
  as effective communicators, 128–131, 134–135
  empowering others, 44–45, 47, 52–53, 127, 128
  as facilitators, 91–94, 95–96
  feedback for employees, 164, 165–167
  feminine leadership and, 15–26, 18f
  fostering commitment, 136–137f
  groups and, 97–98
  hiring and, 115–123
  as human resources managers, 107–124
  interviewing applicants, 119–123
  leadership and, 8
  maintaining visibility, 114–115
  marketability of, 114
  mentoring team members, 112–113
  motivating others, 54, 156–157
  networking, 30, 113–114
  nurse managers and, 4–5
  overcoming resistance, 83
  performance evaluations and, 159–160, 162–163
  relating to supervisors, 152
  reliability and, 127, 130
  resolving conflict, 102–103
  responsibilities of, 155–156
  as role models, 52, 125, 127–128
  scheduling time, 151–152
  skills and knowledge for, 10
  strategies for, 10–11, 23–24, 26
  teams and, 49–50, 59–60, 62, 66, 71–73
  transforming health care systems, 28
  trustworthiness of, 127
  women's issues and, 22

and work restructuring, 51–53
 see also Leaders; Team members; Teams
Nurse managers, see Managers
Nurse Wages, 178
Nursing
 applying core values to, 2–3
 caring in, 25–26
 marketing philosophy and, 110
 nursing information systems, 173
Nursing applications, 171–172
Nursing information systems (NIS), 173
Nursing Network Forum, 177

O

Ogborn, S. E., 29
Olson, R., 112
Oncken, W., 151
On-line networks, 177
Open-ended questions, 65
Openness, 131
Organizational rules
 playing by, 36–37
 understanding, 19, 36
 for women, 23
Organizations
 linking job applicants to, 119f
 purpose and business of, 111

P

Participation
 feminine leadership and, 20
 promoting in groups, 96–98
Patient-centered care, 58
Patriarchal values, 15
Peak energy cycles, 146–147
Peer time, 151
Performance
 criteria for, 159–160
 incentives for, 168
 motivation and, 156–158
 need to change and, 79
 rewards for, 167–168
Performance evaluations, 10, 11
 as feedback, 163–164
 record keeping and, 164–166
 unacceptable performance, 166–167
Performance management
 defined, 155
 principles of, 159–160
 rewards for performance, 167–168
 unacceptable performance, 166–167
Performance measurement, 155–169
 continuous feedback and, 164–167
 defined, 157
 documenting, 163–165
 elements of, 161–162
 guidelines for planning, 157–158
 job descriptions and, 158–159
 motivation and, 8
 roles and responsibilities for, 155–156
 see also Performance evaluations
Performance reviews, see Performance
  evaluations
Personal Effectiveness Profile, 64f
Personal mission statements, 141, 142f, 153
Peters, T., 60
Planning
 daily, 145–146
 with goals, 143
 performance measurement, 157–158
Please-arrange-to-see-me meetings, 12–13
Policy, 28–41
 advancing initiatives for, 39–40
 influencing, 37–38
Policy checklist, 39
Political action, 48–49
Political behavior, 30
Political skills, 20, 29–30
Politics, 28–41
 basis for, 29–30
 defined, 29
Positive interactions, 128
Posner, B., 5, 126
Power, 28–41
 acquiring, 31–32
 changing distribution of, 21–23
 conveying personal, 33–34
 defined, 28, 29
 empowerment and, 43–44
 feminine leadership and, 18f, 21–23
 sharing, 21
Power brokers, 35–36
Power structure, 19, 35
Precursor function, 77
Principles
 as basis for leadership, 2
 of change, 76
Priorities
 balancing by nurse leaders, 3
 categorizing, 146–147

Priorities *(continued)*
   daily, 147–148
   evaluating, 153
   saving time with, 149–150, 153
   setting goals, 141–143, 142*f*
   for work, 92
Problem solving
   analysis of problem, 181
   as conflict resolution, 102
   during change, 85–86
   empowerment and, 44
   process of, 86, 88–89*f*
   solutions and, 181–183
   in workplace, 132–135
Problem statements, 180–181, 183
Procedural changes, 85
Professional development, 45–46
Progress reports, 11
Putnam, A., 43

Q

Questions
   for interviewing, 120–122
   open-ended, 65
   resolving conflict and, 103
   types of, 96

R

Recognition, team management and, 71
Record keeping, performance evaluations and, 164–166
Relationships
   feminine leadership and, 17, 18*f*
   fostered by leaders, 4
   as influence on groups, 93
Reliability, 127, 130
Research publications and databases, 178
Reshaping leadership, 25
Resistance, 77, 80, 83, 133
Responsibilities
   assigning during change, 78
   motivation and, 54
   of nurse leaders, 155–156
   of team members, 156
Results, 21, 24
Resumés, 115–117, 116*f*, 117*f*, 177
Rewards
   for achieving goals, 143
   encouraging personal best with, 8
   for performance, 167–168
   team management and, 72
Risk taking, 50, 53
Robert, Cavett, 125
Role models, 52, 125, 127–128
Roles
   of leaders, 9–10
   mastery of and teamwork, 62
   of nurse leaders, 155–156
   of team members, 156
   for women, 22

S

Saving time, 148–150
Scheduling meetings, 12–13
Self-assessment, 108–109
Self-awareness, 127
Self-directed teams, 49–50, 52
Self-image, 33–34
Self-knowledge skills, 2–3
Self-management, 8
Self-reliance, 4
Shared governance model, 46
Sheehan, J., 76
Shifting mind-sets, 84
Silber, M., 82
Sit-down meetings, 12
Skepticism, 132
Smith, D., 65
Solutions, 181–183
Spider web model, 16, 17
Stand-up meetings, 12
Stengel, Casey, 57
Strategic issues, 77
Sturdivant, 109–110
Summarizing, 132
Supervisors, 152
Support
   building atmosphere of, 126–128
   networking as, 30–31
   for performance measurement, 162–163

T

Tagiuri, R., 9
Tannenbaum, R., 52–53
Tarule, J. M., 20
Taylor-Moss, M., 19–20

Team leaders, 62, 66–68, 130–132
Team management, 62, 71–72
Team members
  acknowledging boundaries with, 131
  assessing skills of, 108
  as audiences, 129–130
  behaviors of, 67
  challenging, 54
  change process and, 78
  coaching, 164–165
  creating performance standards, 159–160
  delegating to, 149
  empowering, 42, 43–44, 127–128
  empowerment model and, 46–47
  evaluating nurse leaders, 163
  evaluations of, 159–160
  mentoring of, 112–113
  nurturing career development of, 112
  partnerships with nurse leaders, 108–109
  patient-centered care and, 58
  phases in becoming a, 68–69
  rewarding, 167–168
  roles and responsibilities of, 156
  self-directed teams and, 49–50
  shared governance model and, 46
  sharing control, 48–49
  sharing expertise, 53
  time for, 151
  and work restructuring, 51–53
Team performance worksheet, 70f
Teams
  barriers to developing, 69
  building, 25, 65, 66, 70–71
  coaching, 50
  creating, 49–50, 59–60
  decision making by, 49
  defined, 65
  effectiveness of, 57–58
  empowerment and, 54
  establishing nursing, 58–59
  evaluating, 70
  managing, 62, 71–72
  nurse leader evaluations, 163
  performance measurements for, 163
  preparing members for change, 79–80
  readiness of, 66, 67f
  self-directed teams, 49–50, 52
Teamwork, 57–73
  allocating managerial time for, 59
  benefits of, 67–70
  commitment and, 63, 70–71
  encouraging, 21
  patient-centered care and, 58
  techniques for creating, 49–50, 59–60
Technical skills, 108
Telnet, 176
Time log, 139–140, 140f
Time management, 139–154
  calendars and, 145–146, 145f
  focus and, 141, 149–150
  goals and, 141–145, 142f, 144f
  keeping-track process, 139
  management time, 151
  peak energy cycles and, 146–147
  personal mission statements, 141, 142f, 153
  priorities, 146–150, 153
  saving time, 148–150
  scheduling meetings and, 12–13, 150, 151–152
  staying on track, 152–153
  time log, 139–140, 140f
  time wasters, 147–148
  timekeepers, 100
  tips for, 150
Time savers, 148–150
Time wasters, 147–148
Timekeeper, 100
To-do lists, 145–146
Training programs, 78
Trust
  communicating, 82
  leadership and, 2, 10
  teams and, 63
  in workplace, 135
Trustworthiness, 127

U

Ulrich, B., 147
Understanding, 11
University of Maryland School of Nursing, 177

V

Values
  core, 2–3, 19–20
  feminine, 19–20
  of health care industry, 15
  introducing new, 52
  of women, 20

Vance, C., 112
Visibility, 114–115
Vision
    change and, 80
    communicating to staff, 11–12
    creating a, 60–62
    established by leaders, 4, 5
    making realities from, 40
    role of leaders and, 53
    team management and, 62
    of team member, 107
Visualization, 143
Vogt, J., 54
Voice, 131

W

Wages, 178
Walker, B., 80
Wass, D., 151
Wellins, R. S., 49
Wendt, R., 168
Wheeler, C. E., 44
Wilson, J. M., 49
Women
    effectiveness of, 25
    in health care industry, 23
    leadership and, 16, 17
    values of, 20
    in work force, 22
Women's issues, nurse leaders and, 22
Work
    evaluating performance, 161–162
    priorities for, 92
    restructuring, 51–53
Workplace, 125–138
    communications for supportive, 128–132
    databases on, 177
    enthusiasm in, 21
    fostering commitment in, 136–137f
    as influence on groups, 92
    leadership and, 125–128
    motivation factors in workplace, 70, 71f
    political behavior and, 30
    problem solving in, 132–135
    trust in, 135
    understanding political structure of, 35
Workplace Advocacy Information Database (WAID), 177
World Wide Web (WWW), 176
Writing resumés, 116